Getting
Back to the
TABLE

Getting
Back to the
TABLE

5 STEPS TO REVIVING
STALLED NEGOTIATIONS

Joshua N. Weiss, PhD

Berrett–Koehler Publishers, Inc.

Berrett-Koehler Publishers, Inc.
1333 Broadway, Suite P100
Oakland, CA 94612-1921
Tel: (510) 817-2277
Fax: (510) 817-2278
bkconnection.com

ORDERING INFORMATION

Quantity sales. Special discounts are available on quantity purchases by corporations, associations, and others. For details, please go to bkconnection.com to see our bulk discounts or contact bookorders@bkpub.com for more information.

Individual sales. Berrett-Koehler publications are available through most bookstores. They can also be ordered directly from Berrett-Koehler: Tel: (800) 929-2929; Fax: (802) 864-7626; bkconnection.com.

Orders for college textbook / course adoption use. Please contact Berrett-Koehler: Tel: (800) 929-2929; Fax: (802) 864-7626.

Distributed to the US trade and internationally by Penguin Random House Publisher Services.

Berrett-Koehler and the BK logo are registered trademarks of Berrett-Koehler Publishers, Inc.

Printed in the United States of America

Berrett-Koehler books are printed on long-lasting acid-free paper. When it is available, we choose paper that has been manufactured by environmentally responsible processes. These may include using trees grown in sustainable forests, incorporating recycled paper, minimizing chlorine in bleaching, or recycling the energy produced at the paper mill.

Library of Congress Cataloging-in-Publication Data
Names: Weiss, Joshua N., author.
Title: Getting back to the table : 5 steps to reviving stalled negotiations / Joshua N. Weiss, PhD.
Description: First edition. | Oakland, CA : Berrett-Koehler Publishers, [2025] | Includes bibliographical references and index.
Identifiers: LCCN 2024037808 (print) | LCCN 2024037809 (ebook) | ISBN 9798890570468 (paperback) | ISBN 9798890570475 (pdf) | ISBN 9798890570482 (epub)
Subjects: LCSH: Negotiation. | Negotiation in business.
Classification: LCC BF637.N4 W4573 2025 (print) | LCC BF637.N4 (ebook) | DDC 658.4/052—dc23/eng/20241114
LC record available at https://lccn.loc.gov/2024037808
LC ebook record available at https://lccn.loc.gov/2024037809

First Edition

32 31 30 29 28 27 26 25 24   10 9 8 7 6 5 4 3 2 1

Book production: Happenstance Type-O-Rama
Cover design: Ashley Ingram

*This book is dedicated to my father,
Dr. Earle Weiss, who has taught me the tremendous
value of being a lifelong learner. He has shown
me the critical importance of being resilient in
the face of life's failures and difficulties and having
persistence toward your goals. Thank you, Dad.*

CONTENTS

Preface. ix

INTRODUCTION: Negotiation Failure, Resilience,
and the 5 Steps 1

CHAPTER 1: Negotiation Failures and Their Magnitude 13

CHAPTER 2: What Gets in the Way of Learning from
Negotiation Failure?. 33

CHAPTER 3: Overview: You Failed, Now What? 43

CHAPTER 4: Step 1: You Failed—Accept It. 49

CHAPTER 5: Step 2: Analyze the Forest and the Trees—
What Went Wrong?. 59

CHAPTER 6: Step 3: Not Just Any Lessons—
Learn the Right Ones 75

CHAPTER 7: Step 4: Actively Unlearn What Your
Weaknesses Taught You 87

CHAPTER 8: Step 5: Return to the Table Smarter
and Stronger. 107

CHAPTER 9: Looking Back to Look Ahead 121

Appendix A: Additional Biases 125

Appendix B: Improvisation Games. 129

Notes. 135

Acknowledgments 143

Index 145

About the Author 153

PREFACE

In a previous book I authored, I focused on successful cases of negotiation. Many readers gave me wonderful feedback about the book, but one person stopped me in my tracks with what they had to say. The woman I was speaking with told me how much she'd enjoyed the book and its real-world applicability, but then she asked me a question that rattled around in my brain for quite some time: Why did I focus on successes? As she explained, "When I look back at my negotiations, I remember the successes fondly. However, the real lessons that I have learned throughout my career from a negotiation point of view have come from my failures." Then she asked, "Have you considered another book focused on failure and what we can really learn from those processes to help us grow and become better negotiators?" In the moment I blurted out, "No, but I will consider it!" After contemplating the question for some time, and running the idea by other people in the field of negotiation, I decided it would indeed be a worthwhile endeavor . . . hence this book.

To be perfectly frank with you, my own life has been riddled with failure. I was not a great student as a child, in high school, or at university (I finally figured it all out in graduate school). I was a decent but not outstanding athlete, despite putting in a lot of time and effort and a desire to be great. I was a slightly better than average violinist as a child, but I didn't practice the way I needed to in order to excel because I didn't have the passion for it. In other words, at an early age, and indeed through my early twenties, I failed at many things. Interestingly, over time, those failures turned out to have been more of a blessing than a curse. You see, when you fail and you survive to talk about it, you learn valuable lessons about what to do the next time, and why. Further, from a psychological point of view, if you understand that failure is part of life, the pressure falls away, because you know it will happen. You don't strive to fail, of course, but you do accept it as part of the overall journey of life.

The same is true when it comes to negotiation. Failure is, simply put, part of the landscape. While that may be daunting for some, it may come as a relief to others. As an example of what I mean, while I was working on this book I shared with one of my students that I was writing a book on failure in negotiation and how to learn from it. She looked at me and said, "Oh, thank God!" Curious, I replied, "Why do you say that?" She elaborated further, "I feel as though all we read and hear about in the program are the negotiation successes. As a student of negotiation, this view makes me feel as though I have to be perfect and always succeed. If I'm not always doing really well, I must be doing something very wrong. I'm glad that's not the case!"

It certainly is *not* the case, and I hope that some candor from me will set the record straight for that student and others in the field. We have to humanize the process for everyone and help negotiators understand that failure is something they will encounter and have to grapple with as part of becoming more effective. The question ultimately is, what do you do with that failure when it transpires?

Consider the world of startup businesses. Before you read the next sentence, pause and ask yourself: What would I guess is the success rate of this type of company? The answer is 10%, which means that 90% of startups fail.[1] And yet, many thousands of startups attempt to get off the ground worldwide every year. Now, while I certainly don't believe the success rate is nearly that low in negotiation, failure is definitely part of the equation. When it happens for startup entrepreneurs, they have to cope with it, learn from it, be resilient, and get back to the drawing board with a new idea that just might take hold—having learned some valuable lessons from their last failed endeavor. The same is true in negotiation.

This book is about that process. The aim of focusing on failure is not to apportion blame or second-guess what could have, or should have, been done. In fact, as I will explain later, that way of thinking is one of the most significant blocks to truly learning from our failures. And that's the real goal—to learn from those failures and to come back to the table wiser and a better negotiator than before. To that end, I have developed a framework that I believe negotiators will be able to systematically follow to do just that.

My plea to you is this: Embrace your failures, cope with the losses associated with them, understand why they happened so you can genuinely learn from them, get back to the table, and continue on your pursuit to be the best negotiator you can be.

—JOSHUA N. WEISS

Introduction
Negotiation Failure, Resilience, and the 5 Steps

Only those who dare to fail greatly,
can ever achieve greatly.

—ROBERT F. KENNEDY[1]

Negotiation Failure

A survey of the literature on negotiation produces something very interesting—a lot of discussion about success. To give just a few examples, books on the topic include Herb Cohen's *You Can Negotiate Anything: How to Get What You Want*, Tim Castle's *The Art of Negotiation: How to Get What You Want (Every Time)*, and Peter B. Stark and Jane Flaherty's *The Only Negotiating Guide You Will Ever Need: 101 Ways to Win Every Time in Any Situation*. These book titles make a lot of sense, because everyone wants to succeed in their negotiations. But while that may be our ultimate goal, it is simply not how negotiation works in practice. While negotiators always strive to succeed, Kennedy's words are prescient. We all experience failure . . . especially given the complexity of many of our negotiations.

Some of the most difficult conversations I have with people when it comes to negotiation are around failure. That is because negotiating effectively, with all its barriers and pitfalls, is very difficult. The dilemma we face when we fail is that we have to figure out what to do in the aftermath. How do we understand what happened? How much of the failure was due to our actions, and how do we cope with that? What about the other negotiator and their contributions? And how much of the failure was due to hidden dimensions and a lack of certain information that was not known or available at the outset? Negotiation is a multifaceted mix of the participants' actions and reactions, dealing with incomplete information, and numerous additional dynamics, some of which are in our control and some of which are not. So, we *will* fail. The key question is, how do we become resilient in the face of these failures and use them as an opportunity to grow and get better at this craft?

Before continuing, let me share with you how I define the purpose of negotiation, because I have a rather broad conception of the process. We generally negotiate to do one of three things. First, we negotiate to *create a deal*—perhaps between two businesses where one provides a service to the other, or a union and management trying to agree on a contract that benefits them both, or governments crafting a free trade pact. Second, we use negotiation to *build relationships and partnerships* with those we want to engage with, for various reasons, now and into the future. Parents and teachers who work together as part of a parent–teacher organization negotiate much more effectively if they have a strong relationship with each other, and the governments of states that border one another and engage regularly on many fronts can collaborate most effectively in their negotiations with a positive rapport. Finally, we use negotiation to *solve conflicts or have difficult conversations*. Whether internally with co-workers or externally with clients, our working lives are filled with conflicts. The process of, and skill sets associated with negotiation, lend themselves to dealing with these kinds of challenges—particularly when the human element (i.e., issues related to respect, our identity, etc.) is involved.

Now that we know when we use negotiation, let me share my experience of a negotiation situation that occurred many years ago in which I failed. It was a difficult pill to swallow, because I made a mistake that I could likely have avoided. A consulting job was offered to me that was very generous in terms of salary, but there was an important sticking point. The company wanted me to commute close to two hours every day, and I simply did not want to do that because I had small children at the time and did not want to miss that much time with them. I explained to the company that I was prepared to come in two days each week, or perhaps three occasionally, if it was really necessary. There seemed to be many ways to handle the situation, and I tried to offer some creative ideas, as did they, but none of them stuck. We went back and forth to no avail, until we collectively gave up on the process. Only later did I learn that the company ultimately hired someone else for the position and gave them more flexibility than they were prepared to give to me. Part of that had to do with the person's level of experience, but part had to do with the company's interests. It turned out that I had misunderstood one of their underlying requirements: for the person they hired to be present for all high-profile events, but not necessarily every day. Somehow that distinction never crystalized clearly in our conversations, so we were unable to settle on a viable solution that would have benefitted both them and me.

In the end, not only did we fail to reach an agreement, but damage was done to the relationship in the process. I was disappointed on a number of fronts, and I was concerned about my reputation and how it would be impacted, given the stature of this organization in the field. I happened to speak to a colleague after all this transpired, and he said something to me that I will never forget: "Once you realize you are not nearly as important as you think you are, you will be able to handle your failures a lot better." It was tough advice, but he was absolutely right. I had failed, but the company—and for that matter, the world—had moved on and hardly noticed. I needed to as well, but first I had to try to determine what had gone wrong and why. What I also came to understand was that very few knew that I had failed; it was me that was dwelling on it. That story has stayed front and center in my mind all these years.

I've noticed that people generally seem to have one of three responses to failure in negotiation when it happens. Recall the famous children's fairy tale *Goldilocks and the Three Bears*, written by Robert Southey. As the story goes, Goldilocks finds an empty house in the woods after getting lost. She's very hungry, and when she enters the house, she notices three bowls of porridge. The first bowl of porridge is too hot, and the second is too cold, but the third is just right. We can draw an analogy to the three types of responses to failure in negotiation.

The first response, what I would deem one that is "too hot," is denial and rationalization. From this perspective, a negotiator says to themselves, "Yes, I failed to meet my objectives, but it wasn't my fault. The other person is to blame; if they had just done X, Y, or Z, we wouldn't have ended up here." The negotiator with this narrative does not take anything away from their failure because they are too busy trying to protect their reputation and blaming the failure on the other negotiator or circumstances out of their control. When they go back to the table, they do so with overconfidence and are likely to make the same mistakes, having learned very little from their previous experiences.

The second response, what I would deem "too cold," is for the negotiator to put all the onus on themselves for the failure. The experience is so debilitating and, frankly, humiliating that they really don't want to negotiate again. If they do go back to the negotiation table, they do so with tremendous anxiety and a lack of confidence in their ability. Typically, this response leads to a destructive cycle of failure, fear/anxiety, more failure, and so on.

The third response, which is the "just right" approach, lies at the heart of this book. What does the just right approach look like? In general, a negotiator understands and accepts that failure is a possible outcome of negotiation. Then, when failure happens, they face that cold, hard reality and begin to deal with it. After coping with the failure, they move into a process of trying to understand what happened. This means thinking about the lessons they can learn, the mistakes they may have made that contributed to the failure, and why they made those mistakes in the first place. Inevitably, this leads to the idea of thinking about what they can *unlearn* so they don't make the same errors again. And finally, they pick up their seat at the table that had fallen over due to their failure, stand it upright, sit back down, and get back to negotiating. All of this requires resilience and a recognition that being a great negotiator is a journey of continual learning.

Becoming a Resilient Negotiator

I mentioned earlier that I failed in a particular negotiation, and the experience stuck with me. It was really at that point that I learned the value of becoming a resilient negotiator, able to get back up, dust myself off, learn from my failure, and get back to the table, having taken away something important for the future. But it was that idea of learning from my failure that I kept returning to. How do we, in the field of negotiation, really learn when we fail to meet our objectives? And what is really needed in this most difficult of undertakings to do so effectively?

It's all well and good to want to be a resilient negotiator and to be able to get back to the table, but if you lack the right mindset, knowledge, skills, and confidence, you won't get there. Let me unpack these dimensions of resilience as a precursor to our discussion of negotiation failure and how to learn from it.

It is imperative to begin with our mindset, because that is where so much of our resilience and ability to deal with failure comes from. Let's start with the idea of "fixed" and "growth" mindsets.[2] When I first learned of this concept it was an epiphany for me, and it helped me to articulate to people the downside of a fixed view of our abilities and the upside of a growth outlook. Briefly, the progenitor of the idea, Carol Dweck, explains the distinction this way: "Individuals who believe their talents can be developed (through hard work, good strategies, and input from others) have a growth mindset. They tend to achieve more than those with a fixed mindset (those who believe their talents are innate gifts). This is because they worry less about looking smart and put more energy into learning."[3] It should be fairly evident why this is so critical when it comes to failure, resilience, and negotiation.

The growth mindset connects directly to our ability to be resilient by helping us convince ourselves that with enough knowledge, skill development, and ability, we can ultimately succeed. We then focus on what we need to do to improve instead of on blaming the other or thinking we can't do something because, well, we're just not good at it and never will be. Our mindset becomes, "If I work hard enough, I can do things I never imagined were possible."

Developing a growth mindset is not easy. It requires not only knowing our strengths and building on them, but more importantly, understanding our weaknesses, embracing them, and working diligently to improve them. I also learned this lesson the hard way in a scenario involving my oldest daughter. When she was growing up, she struggled with math. At one point, early on in her struggles, I told her that she should not feel bad because I was never great at the subject, and she'd probably inherited that lack of ability from me. That was a fixed perspective, and it was exactly the *wrong* thing to say to her. I was trying to make her feel better, but what I really did was debilitate her and make her think that it was normal that she was not good at math, there was nothing she could do about it, and she should just give up. When I learned about the growth mindset, I immediately thought of this example and, candidly, felt a deep sense of remorse.

So, I went back to my daughter and told her that I had given her very bad advice and was wrong to have done so. She was very surprised to hear this from her father, but it was the truth, and I had to own it. Ever since then, with her and my two other daughters, my message has been: "When you work hard, you can do things you never thought you could." Thankfully, they have embraced that message and gone on to overcome many obstacles. When I see them slipping back toward a fixed mindset, I do my best to push them back toward a growth mindset because I know how destructive the former can be.

Let me give you another example of where this comes up a lot in my teaching, training, coaching, practice, and advising work. The ability to think quickly on one's feet and adapt is a valuable attribute to possess in negotiation, since we are always working with incomplete information. When I bring up the essentiality of this skill to my different audiences, there are invariably people who say something like, "Oh, I'm not good at that. I can't do it. I freeze up and my mind locks. Sorry. What else can I try, since I can't do that?" The answer I offer them, which they generally really don't want to hear, is that there is no substitute for this skill and they have to find a way to learn it. But I don't stop there—I then do two things in collaboration with them. I begin by asking them *why* they don't think they can learn to think on their feet, and then we work on the specific challenge(s) they face. It could be a lack of confidence, or that their job requires a lot of planning, or that they grew up in a family where everything was carefully planned, and without that process, they feel lost. Once we get to the root of the problem, we work to improve upon it. Next, we practice, practice, then practice some more. Slowly they make progress, to a point where they let go of their fixed mindset, gain confidence through their actions as they witness that they *can* get better at adapting, and start focusing on how to grow their ability to overcome this challenge.

The next components that we need to become resilient in the realm of negotiation are knowledge and skills. Without knowledge and the necessary skill set, we have little hope of succeeding in negotiation, particularly when things become difficult. While there is some variance in what people in the field view as the core skills of negotiation, from my perspective the following are at the heart of being effective:

- Problem solving
- Assertiveness
- Empathy
- Analysis and preparation
- Having difficult conversations

- Dealing with difficult people
- Emotional intelligence
- Persuasion and influence

There are lots of books, articles, and training courses available on how to master these skills. However, I would argue that this is only one piece of the puzzle—we also must have general knowledge about strategy, key concepts, and critical dynamics that impact the process. Again, there are many courses and degree programs as well as books and podcasts that can help you acquire this knowledge. The bottom line is that negotiation, like other realms, must be studied in depth and be viewed as a process of continual learning and growth.

Confidence in negotiation is another key part of the equation, and it's a quality that can be elusive. Depending on where a discussion progresses in a negotiation, we may have more or less confidence based on our knowledge level. When we're in a realm where we lack knowledge, we often lose confidence and are more vulnerable to making a mistake. When we move back to a realm where we are knowledgeable, we feel our confidence flowing back. This ebb and flow is an important aspect in most negotiations and is something we have to manage, but we can improve our confidence as our knowledge grows and we learn from our failures. I'll come back to this idea later in the book and share more information on how to do this most effectively.

A Pre-Step, Followed by the 5 Steps

Now that we have established that resilience is the foundation for handling failure in negotiation, we can build on that footing by gaining a deeper understanding of the types and magnitudes of failures we might face. This will be the topic of Chapter 1, and we'll follow that in Chapter 2 by examining the potential barriers to truly learning from these failures. These chapters are an essential pre-step to the 5 steps for getting back to the table that are outlined in the rest of the book. Honestly, as a reader you might not enjoy these first few chapters, because nobody truly enjoys examining their setbacks and failures in the way that we will. However, we simply can't progress as negotiators without this knowledge and thorough examination. This part of the book will be the most challenging for many readers, but it is imperative that we push ourselves by turning the mirror inward.

We will then make a shift to the aforementioned 5-step process, so we have a framework from which to learn and to master over time. This is the missing piece for so many of the people I have spoken with, from whom I hear, "I failed—now what? I don't really know what to do to make sense of it all!"

The 5-step process will help you answer the following questions:

- ▣ What do I do when I have failed?
- ▣ How do I really learn from what happened, so I don't make those mistakes in future negotiations and I become a better negotiator in the end?
- ▣ If it is still possible, how do I get back to the table in a particular negotiation that failed but is still very important to me?

Here is a very short preview of the steps, and a bit about their sequence. The first step in the process is to accept the failure and cope with it. For most of us this may very well be the most challenging of the 5 steps, because of what we believe it says about us to ourselves and to others. However, as much as we might like this to be a completely logical and rational process, it is not. There is a strong emotional component that must be addressed initially in order for a negotiator to be in the right mental space to then work through the next steps in the process.

The second step is to conduct a deep dive into what happened and why, examining both the Forest and the Trees from an analytical point of view. The Forest is the big picture. It is valuable to start our analysis here and try to get an accurate perspective of what really happened at this level. Too often, we dive quickly into the details and miss some big-picture items. When we have done the Forest analysis accurately, this will give us a stronger foundation to look at the Trees (i.e., the details), carefully assessing our micro behaviors and the individual decisions that led us to the setback or failure.

Following that probing, the third step is learning lessons— the correct ones—from our failure. There are many lessons from a failed negotiation that are critical to grasp, but there is a very important distinction to be made here: Unless we are very careful it is easy to learn the wrong lessons from our failures, which in turn will give us a false sense of comfort. That will set us up for problems in the future. Instead, in this step we must really hone in on learning the *right* lessons and when they may or may not be applicable in our upcoming negotiations. To enable this it's important to be aware of what dimensions to compare between negotiations, such as the number of negotiating parties, negotiation styles, and dynamics, including time and time pressure, power, generations, gender, and culture. That way, we can be sure we are comparing apples to apples and not apples to watermelons.

Once we have done this critical learning, the fourth step is about actively unlearning the things that led to our failure. The thinking and behaviors we must unlearn are more broadly connected to our weaknesses in negotiation. When we actively unlearn the things that caused us the problem, we create new space to learn innovative ways of thinking and approaching negotiation differently.

The last step in the process is returning to the table smarter and stronger thanks to the knowledge we have gained. As in many fields, knowledge breeds confidence, and this process will help us build our negotiation competence slowly and surely. We will also learn how to deal with the uncertainty of the process and discover ways of becoming more adaptable, so we can maintain our confidence throughout as much of the negotiation as possible. With this 5-step process in mind, when failures happen in the future in the course of our negotiation endeavors, we will know what to do to deal with them and how to really learn from them.

Finally, let me be clear about what is meant by *getting back to the table*. There are actually two meanings to this term, depending on the circumstances. The first is when a failure has happened, but the door has not been completely shut on that specific negotiation process. There is an opportunity, albeit not an easy path, to get back to the table to continue negotiating. In this case, getting back to the table is much more focused on the near term and a specific negotiation process. The second meaning of getting back to the table has to do with the longer term. If we have failed, the door is closed, and no further negotiations are going to happen in this particular instance, how do we truly learn from what happened so we can grow and develop as a negotiator in the future? The quest to be the best negotiator possible requires this type of reflection and in-depth examination. So, let's get started!

1

Negotiation Failures and Their Magnitude

Generally speaking, when it comes to failure in negotiation most people want to know two things: what are the different ways I can fail, and how bad is it going to be? Before we get to those two core questions, let's briefly define what we mean by failure in this context—even though that may seem obvious to some. For the purposes of this book, failure is defined as *not meeting the objective or goal delineated at the outset of the negotiation process.*

Now, some people question whether there is such a thing as failure in negotiation, claiming that any failure is merely a setback or a stepping stone on the way to success. I think it's important to state clearly that I believe negotiation failure is a real thing, although I do sincerely believe that these failures ultimately can lead us to success in the long term, if we manage them properly and learn from them. In my mind, there is absolutely nothing wrong with recognizing a failure for what it is, and indeed it is vital that we do so, so we can cope with it and address it. Facing the cold, hard facts about negotiation failures may not be easy, but it's important, for a myriad of reasons we will discuss throughout the book.

What happens if we avoid calling not meeting our goal in negotiation a failure? This is an interesting question and one that is worth grappling with briefly. The answer, often, is that we gloss over what happened, and we neglect to be honest with ourselves about what transpired and what we could have done differently. Consider this example. After his team the Milwaukee Bucks—the top seed in the Eastern Conference of the National Basketball Association (NBA) playoffs—lost to the lowest-seeded Miami Heat in the first round in April 2023, a reporter asked star player Giannis Antenakupo if he viewed the season as a failure. Giannis was praised for his answer: "Do you get a promotion every year, in your job? No, right? So, every year you work is a failure? Yes, or no? No. Every year you work, you work toward something, towards a goal, which is to get a promotion, to be able to take care of your family, provide a house for them or take care of your parents. You work towards a goal—it's not a failure. It's steps to success. There's always steps to it. Michael Jordan played 15 years, won six championships. The other nine years was a failure? That's what you're telling me?"[1]

I appreciate the positive outlook, and in the long term, he may well be correct. However, Antenakupo's inability to own the failure has a downside. Alternatively, he might have stated: "We failed this year. Our goal was to win a championship, and we did not do that. I will say, we learned some important lessons in terms of what it is going to take to win a title, and that is what we are ultimately aiming for in the future." The difference is subtle, but important. Put differently: Don't deny failure. Own it.

For most of us, failure in negotiation is something we dread because of the consequences that follow, but it is also something that many of us are only too familiar with from our past experiences. None of us ever sets out to fail, but we subconsciously realize that failures are bound to happen—particularly, as Kennedy reminded us earlier, when we really challenge ourselves to do something new, creative, and difficult. In other words, failure is part of the negotiation terrain, so we'd better get used to it and figure out how best to deal with it and, crucially, learn from it so we can continue to grow and become more effective negotiators.

You might be wondering, can we really isolate the cause of a failure in negotiation when there are so many dynamics at play? From my perspective, the way to approach this question is "Yes, and . . ." What I mean by this is that when we look back at our negotiations where we experienced significant setbacks or failed, we can often identify a primary cause. Of course, it is also important to account for secondary causes, or exacerbating factors, that may have played a role as well. These are not the essence of the problem, but they will have added to the challenge and made it that much more difficult to deal with. With this in mind, let's delve into the categories of failure and their magnitude.

Categories of Failure

In my experience as a negotiator, I have identified seven primary types of negotiation failure. While I do not pretend that this is an exhaustive or definitive list, it can provide a useful framework for analysis. As you read through this list, think about your own experiences with failure and which of these categories they might fit into.

1. Take a Crack at It Failure

When the negotiation challenge is very difficult, but you try anyway and expect to fail in the short term

This type of failure is the least problematic; it occurs when we know that failure is actually more likely than success in the short term, but there's a strong opportunity to learn from the experience. This is often the case when we are trying to push the envelope or looking for a breakthrough when faced with a very difficult negotiation issue.[2]

We most commonly see this type of failure when it comes to negotiating internally about the development of new and innovative products—some of which may have a significant societal impact. The story of Steve Jobs and the iPhone fits this description. According to Brian Merchant, author of the book *The One Device: The Secret History of the iPhone*, Apple's founder, Jobs, was initially very reluctant to develop the product. The engineers knew they had something good, but they had to convince Jobs first. As Merchant describes it, "They knew there was a right way to approach Jobs with this stuff and there was a wrong way, and you had to, sort of very strategically roll it out and give it to the right person to give it to him on the right day when he was in the right mood."[3] They found their intermediary in Apple's design chief, Jonathan Ive. Ive said to the team, "Let me bring it to Jobs when he is in a good mood, when, you know, the time is right."

Ive was one of Jobs' closest friends, but when he unveiled the project and attempted to negotiate to produce a prototype, Jobs wasn't impressed; according to Merchant, he simply "said 'Meh.' And, just kind of, you know, wrote the idea off." The engineers, however, were persistent, going through tests and failures and more tests and more failures until they got the new touchscreen technology just right. Then they brought it back to Jobs to negotiate with him again. Merchant summarizes the interaction this way: "Sure enough, Jobs came around. He thought about it some more. He asked to see the demo again and he said, 'OK, this is pretty cool.' And then fast forward a couple weeks, couple months and he loves it. And now he is like, 'Oh, you know what? Multi-touch? Yeah, I invented that.'"[4] In this case, the engineering team knew at the outset that this type of failure in their negotiations was part of the process and recognized that they would likely have to negotiate many times with Jobs before he might say yes.

2. Slipping Through Our Fingers Failure

Not reaching agreement when it is eminently possible

The next type of failure is called the Slipping Through Our Fingers failure. Why? Because when something slips through our fingers, it was within our grasp, and, somehow, we let it slip away. In other words, we did not reach an agreement that was achievable and would have met the parties' respective interests and needs when it was very possible to do so.

Let me explain why I include these two caveats. With regard to the first one, there are many instances where a possible deal is on the table, but for one reason or another it is not achievable. For example, what one party is asking of the other may simply not be possible, or the timing might not be right, causing negotiations to stall or parties to come to the table in bad faith, or the resources to make a deal work might not exist.

Regarding the second proviso, it's important to keep in mind that the purpose of negotiation is not simply to reach an agreement; it is to meet our goals and needs as best as possible. If a possible deal is on the table but for some reason is not achieved, it only qualifies as a failure if that deal would have met our objectives. (If we reach an agreement that doesn't satisfy our underlying interests, that's another form of failure, which we'll look at next.)

Let's consider an example that illustrates this type of failure. Jon Lester was a Major League Baseball player for the Boston Red Sox. After being drafted, he made his way to the team in summer 2006. Tragically, in September of that same year Lester was diagnosed with anaplastic large cell lymphoma. Fortunately for Lester, this form of high-grade lymphoma typically has a favorable clinical course—as it ultimately did for him. The Red Sox stood by him and his family through this arduous and trying journey. In 2007, he was back pitching for the Red Sox and was integral to the team winning the World Series.

Fast-forward to January 2014, when Lester was to become a free agent the following season. He emphatically stated at the time, "These guys are my No. 1 priority . . . I want to be here until they have to rip this jersey off my back."[5] Lester added that he expected to get a lower offer to sign an extension with the Red Sox than he might get elsewhere, and that he was willing to take the hit. In his words, "I understand that you're going to take a discount to stay. Do I want to do that? Absolutely." He finished by uttering, "But just like they want it to be fair for them, I want it to be fair for me and my family." And that is where the negotiation problem began.

The Red Sox made Lester what they likely considered an "initial offer to get the conversation started"—a four-year, $70 million proposal. Arguably, the market or industry standard for Lester, when looking at comparable pitchers, was more along the lines of five to six years and between $120 and $150 million. Unbeknownst to Lester, the Red Sox were willing to up their offer (eventually raising it to six years and $135 million), but by that time the damage had been done due to the comparatively low early sum. Despite Lester's previous comments about his deep desire to stay in Boston and his willingness to be flexible around the compensation, a negative tone to the negotiation had been set. Both sides expressed a desire to reach a deal, but Lester ultimately ceased negotiations, subsequently asking for, and being granted, a trade to the Oakland Athletics. A year later, he ended up signing a long-term deal with the Chicago Cubs.[6]

This negotiation is a classic example of two parties who had all the makings of an achievable deal, a mutually expressed desire to reach said deal, and other positive dynamics going for them, only to have an agreement slip through their fingers due to multiple factors that, in hindsight, could have been avoided. There is no way to see this process as anything but a failure for both sides.

3. What Were You Thinking Failure

Not meeting one's negotiation objectives/interests

As was previously mentioned, the goal of negotiation is not necessarily just to reach an agreement, but rather for negotiators to meet their objectives and interests as best as possible. Many agreements that are reached fail to meet a negotiator's objectives and, therefore, should be considered failures. In these cases it's fair to ask, "What you were thinking by agreeing to that?" Here is an illustrative case of such a failure.

Maureen worked in sales at Adchips Inc. and was only a few years out of college. She desperately wanted to succeed in her position, which she hoped would serve as a stepping stone to the rest of her career. Maureen's job was to sell microchips to large companies that used them in their technology-related products.

One such company was Teradon, a leader in the industry and an organization Adchips had worked with for some time.

Our story begins when Maureen and her counterpart, Michael, met to engage in a negotiation to renew Teradon's previous contract. Michael had previously dealt with another Adchips salesperson, but that person had recently left to take a position at a different company. Sensing that Maureen was relatively new and a bit inexperienced, Michael asked her for a sizable order of microchips. The order exceeded her goals—but this would come at a cost. He explained that he wanted a 20% discount, given the size of the order and as a reward for the many years Teradon had used Adchips' chips.

Maureen was taken aback by the initial offer. The quantity was fantastic, but by her quick calculations the discount would make this a small downer for her company. Instead of stepping away to consider the deal or making a counteroffer, she negotiated with herself, rationalizing that the former consideration outweighed the latter and that she would be able to explain this to her boss. She agreed to Michael's terms.

After preliminarily signing off on the deal, she took it back to her boss, nervously hoping for approval. Despite giving up a significant percentage to close the deal, she was very excited about the size of the order. Her boss reviewed the agreement and was shocked that Maureen had already signed off on the deal. After running the numbers comprehensively, she showed Maureen how the agreement was even more of a downer for the company than she'd anticipated, due to a lack of inflationary clauses over the life of the four-year contract. Maureen's boss finished the conversation by stating, "What were you thinking? I'm sorry, but this deal is unacceptable. We have to fix this, and it's going to take some serious work." Maureen, feeling humiliated, admitted that she had made a mistake in the calculations and now realized that the agreement did not meet the company's underlying interests and would set it back quite a bit.

In this negotiation, Maureen was able to reach an agreement, but she did not meet her or her company's financial objectives in doing so. As such, this was a failed negotiation that she would have been better off not concluding with an agreement.

4. Penny-Wise and Pound-Foolish Failure

Reaching an agreement that damages the relationship

Some agreements are created in such a manner that they achieve the tangible objective—say, agreeing on a monetary amount—but in doing so they damage the relationship between the parties. The reason this type of failure is called Penny-Wise and Pound-Foolish is because a negotiator who is penny-wise tries to save a small amount in the short term at the expense of the long term. While money is often part of the equation, in this context it is really about emphasizing the short-term gain over the longer-term relationship. Since effective negotiation most often relies on strong relationships, particularly when negotiating with the same person or organization time and again, this form of failure can have lasting consequences.[7]

Here is an archetypal example. A number of years ago, I purchased a used car from a dealership while trading in an older vehicle. I had already bought two cars from this dealer in the past and used them to service my vehicles, so we had developed a solid relationship over time. I was pleased with the deal, except for one thing: the car's tires were quite worn and needed to be replaced. I pointed this out to the salesperson, who said he understood my concern. He then explained that the dealership was running a promotion: with all pre-owned car purchases, new tires would be provided to anyone free of charge within the first year. "Just schedule a time with our service department in the coming weeks," he said, "and they'll take care of it." This seemed reasonable to me, and my previous experiences with the dealership had been positive, so I agreed. Fast-forward a week, and I called to set up a time to have the tires replaced. When I did so, I sought to reaffirm the arrangement so there were no surprises. That's when the difficulties began.

The service technician explained that they had no such deal in their system and could not grant me that arrangement. I asked to be transferred to the salesperson I had worked with. When I got him on the phone, I recounted my experience to him, and he denied ever telling me about the tire deal. We went back and forth, with me pressing him on whether he recalled the conversation and him saying vaguely that he did remember discussing the issue, but he refused to admit to ever having stated anything about a tire deal. I acknowledged that some form of misunderstanding must have occurred and asked if there was anything they were willing to do, given that I had been a very good customer over the years. He said they were willing to give me a 10% discount on the tires to rectify things. Needless to say, I was not really satisfied with that and countered by asking for a 50% discount, which felt fair to me and a seemed like a reasonable split at this juncture. He was not willing to budge.

At this point I'd become very frustrated, and I asked to speak to the general manager at the dealership. When I got the manager on the phone—someone I had not dealt with in the past—I explained my history with the dealership and the current situation. He was empathetic but stated that the salesperson should not have made any such offer. I admitted that it was quite possible there had been some miscommunication, but expressed that I was deeply disappointed with how they were handling this and that I hoped they would live up to the commitment made regarding the tires, or at least share half of the burden. The manager said they would not do anything beyond offering the 10% discount the salesperson had proposed. I remarked that I had been a good customer over the years and explained that this decision would permanently damage our relationship. He accepted that this was a possibility, but said it was something he was willing to live with. I was seriously disappointed; I felt that the experience was unjust and that there was no respect for the customer relationship. In the end, not only did I stop doing business with the dealership, but I shared my experience with others more broadly and even discussed their practices with the state.

In this example, we see a deal that was done that seemed to work for everyone, but when a commitment was made and not kept it ended up permanently damaging the relationship. The dealer opted to focus on the short term and saving some money, rather than the longer term and losing a good customer. This negotiation was clearly a failure for both parties: I did not get the free new tires promised to me and had to pay to replace them, and the dealership lost a valuable customer (and maybe others) as a result of how they handled the negotiation.

5. Bad Agreement Failure

Reaching a bad agreement that is worse than your BATNA (walk-away alternative)[8]

Many agreements that are reached are, simply put, bad, and should never have been consummated. For example, perhaps they don't serve one or both parties' underlying interests, or they miss out on value that could expand the pie, or a deal is reached that is worse than a party's walkaway alternative (aka *Best Alternative to a Negotiated Agreement*, or *BATNA*). Often negotiators reach these types of agreements because they have not done careful preparation, or they feel pressured. Whatever the cause, it is not uncommon for such agreements to fall apart shortly after the ink is dry.

Think about this example, where a lack of preparation and sufficient information led to a series of bad deals that were much worse than the party's BATNA. Brian Epstein grew up in Liverpool, England. His father was a furniture salesman. Epstein first saw the Beatles play in November 1961. At the time, he was running a record store in Liverpool. The story goes that several customers came into his store asking for a single the Beatles had recorded in Germany. Thinking there might be something to this band, he went over to the Cavern Club at lunchtime one day to see for himself. Of course, he was blown away by what he saw. He returned to the club every day for the next three weeks, then approached the band about being their manager.

In January 1962 Epstein and the Beatles signed their first management contract. Epstein negotiated to receive 25% of the Beatles' earnings, which was a very high percentage for his services. As John Lennon later said, "He wanted to manage us and we had nobody better, so we said, 'All right, you can do it.'"[9] Initially, it seemed to the band that the 25% cut was well worth it. Epstein secured them a deal with George Martin at EMI, he helped bring Ringo Starr into the band, and he helped them remake their sound so that their music resonated with mainstream audiences, first in the UK and then around the world.

Then, problems from a negotiation point of view began to emerge and proliferate. Many of the issues had to do with the fact that Epstein failed to adequately prepare and did not know the ins and outs of the music industry and the standards involved. As he openly stated at the time, "I have no musical knowledge, nor do I know very much about show business or the record business. The Beatles are famous because they are good. It was not my managerial cunning."[10] The first deal Epstein negotiated that can only be characterized as an abject failure had to do with the original EMI contract signed with George Martin. This contract gave the Beatles just one penny for every record sold . . . and that penny was split between them! What's more, the royalty rate was reduced for sales outside the UK: the band received just half a penny per single, again split four ways.

While there were a series of other negotiation failures led by Epstein, one that stands out for a clear lack of preparation had to do with the contract he signed on the Beatles' behalf when they filmed the movie *A Hard Day's Night* in 1964. According to sources that represented the studio at the time, they were determined to allow no more than 25% of the profits to go to the Beatles. Epstein walked into the negotiation and assertively declared: "I think you should know that the boys and I will not settle for anything less than 7.5 per cent."[11] The studio readily agreed, and the Beatles were out vast sums of money.

By any measure these were bad deals for the Beatles, but they were even worse when you consider the industry standard and the level of fame the band was quickly achieving. They had a tremendous amount of negotiation leverage to wield, but Epstein failed to meet those possible realities due a lack of knowledge of the music business and negotiation acumen, and a failure to adequately prepare.

6. Emotionally Unintelligent Failure

When emotions are not managed effectively, and the process collapses as a result

Emotions are an age-old challenge for any negotiator. Emotions will always play a role in negotiation, and they can do so in a productive manner if they are brought into the process with some control. But if emotions are not managed effectively, they usually overwhelm negotiators, often leading to an escalation in tension and ultimately a collapse of the process.

A colleague shared with me the following story about a physician who was very famous for doing organ transplants in his country. He had a unique challenge in that he worked part time at a university teaching and research hospital, and part time in private practice. This led to occasional conflicts arising with his university hospital colleagues (including an undertone of jealousy), as well as a possible conflict of interest between his two roles. For example, when an organ became available, how would it be determined who the recipient should be—patients at the university hospital or at his private practice—and, equally importantly, who would get to decide?

The two sides recognized the problem and agreed to come together to try to work out a solution to the issue. Initially, the doctor and his colleagues failed to make noticeable progress, so they brought in a third party to assist them by guiding the process. According to the doctors, this proved to be very helpful, and the parties made considerable strides toward an agreement. They carved out the main parameters, leaving some details to be finalized. One of the most important details to be addressed was when the agreement would take effect. The doctor explained that he would need about 30 days to get the new processes set up in his private practice. The other side agreed to these terms, and the doctor stated that he was prepared to sign.

But just prior to signing, the lawyer for the other doctors, who had been rather hard-nosed throughout the process, asked if he could meet privately with his clients. When they came back to the table, the lawyer explained that they wanted the deal to go into effect in two days. He did not explain why, and refused to share any further information about his clients' reasoning. The doctor was deeply insulted. He stood up, tore up the agreement, explained that what they would have in two days was his resignation, and stormed out of the room. A promising process came to a crashing end.

There are different possible explanations for what caused this failure, but my colleague was clear that uncontrolled emotions had played a large role and ultimately doomed this process. The doctor who stormed out had felt that this final interaction carried a strong odor of distrust. Understandably, he was offended by the last-minute change and lack of explanation, which indicated to him a deep undertone of disrespect.

7. Under the Table Failure

When the parties fail to notice a hidden dynamic or intangible aspect driving the negotiation

In many negotiations, there are often various hidden dynamics and intangible aspects that hinge on a lack of information. These variables, which I like to say live *under the negotiation table* and out of initial sight, can often be the cause of failure. Much of the time this happens because negotiators don't know to look for them, or miss clues that these "under the surface" elements are what are really driving the negotiation. So, they focus their efforts elsewhere and miss dealing with the essence of the challenge. The following is a very good example of this type of problem and how it can cause a failure in the process.

There was a beautiful hotel situated right on the coast in South Africa. The hotel was part of a bundle of properties and businesses owned by the Dube family. The family had two children, Caroline and Martin, who became involved in the business as they got older. Caroline studied and practiced law and brought that skill set to the family business. Her younger brother, Martin, was a rather weaker character, lacking direction and ending up with a drug problem in his youth. He ultimately overcame this, but the process inflicted much pain and anguish on the family and affected their view of his competence.

After sorting out his life and getting married, Martin sought to take his place in the business. However, bad blood simmered under the surface between the siblings, related to their past interactions. This was exacerbated by their respective spouses, who each had little trust in their brother- and sister-in-law and made that clear to their partners.

Their father, John, ultimately decided to give Martin and his wife a try at running the hotel. Encouragingly, they ran the operation quite well. After some time and positive results, Martin began to demand more independence. In fact, he went so far as to say, "I want to move out from under the guise of the family business, and we would like to have the hotel as our own." Martin's proposal to his father was that he sell it to them on very favorable terms. It was at this point that the situation escalated, with Caroline stepping in and saying that she did not want this to happen because the hotel was the crown jewel of the family business. John agreed with Caroline, as did John's wife, Eleanor. John's counterproposal was that the hotel would remain part of the family business, but that Martin and his wife would continue to run it and be given a larger stake in the business, eventually becoming 10% shareholders. Martin rejected the offer, and the family was at an impasse.

It was this point that the family brought in a third party, Allan, to try to help them negotiate a solution. Both Caroline and Martin said they didn't want their spouses involved in the formal process, and Allan agreed to their wishes. This, however, turned out to be a big mistake, because the spouses, through their behind-the-scenes influence on Caroline and Martin, held the key to reaching an agreement. It was that hidden dimension, and the underlying intangible feelings of mistrust and disdain, that caused the family's negotiations to fail. This failure resulted in irreparable damage, with the family remaining badly divided long into the future.

Again, while this is not necessarily an exhaustive list, I consider this a decent overview of the different types of failures that can occur in negotiation. But there's one final dimension to discuss—namely, the magnitude. In other words, exactly how bad was the failure?

Magnitudes of Failure

As we all know, when we negotiate there are bumps in the road. But are those bumps mere potholes that we can fill in and get through with some persistence, or are they more severe, where the entire road needs ripping up and repaving? There is clearly a big difference, which corresponds to the magnitude of the failure we are experiencing in our negotiation. This is something that must be determined as part of the analysis of failure. For example, did the parties set out to explore a difficult negotiation knowing they were unlikely to succeed in this process, but hoping they might learn something that would ultimately help them meet their objectives in the future? Or was the failure a temporary setback, with the parties likely to revive talks in the near future? Or did it go well beyond that, into the realm of a catastrophe that forever destroyed the relationship between the parties and any hope of a successful negotiation? Severity is a continuum, so all of these outcomes (and more) are possible.

To help us understand the nature and seriousness of the failure we are experiencing, I have created a four-level magnitude scale (Figure 1-1) that can help us determine whether it is worth our time and effort to try to revive a specific negotiation or come back to the table and attempt a new negotiation after some time has passed. In most cases the answer will be yes, we should try very hard to get back to the table, but there may be some instances where we have to recognize that the failure we've experienced is beyond repair.

Level I: Intelligent Failure

This first level borrows the concept of *intelligent failure* from Sim Sitkin, who coined the term in his paper "Learning Through Failure: The Strategy of Small Losses."[12] Sitkin defined intelligent failures as failures that are somewhat expected, due to

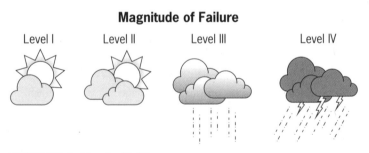

FIGURE 1-1. How bad is it?

the uncertainty of the process and the desire to push the envelope and see what happens, engaging in purposeful exploration that advances an idea or concept. It is anticipated that failure will happen and lead to the next process and potential breakthroughs. In particularly challenging negotiations, we often experience this type of failure because the process itself is an exploration of what is possible. If a process fails—even when creative thinking is involved—and there is something to be learned for future processes, or seeds are planted for the next round of talks, we are working in the realm of intelligent failure and at Level I on our scale. At this level, failure is not necessarily seen as a negative thing.

Level II: Temporary Setback

A failure at this level is the least significant type of negative failure. It manifests itself in the form of a temporary setback or the breakdown of a process, but definitely not a collapse. With this type of failure there is usually a relatively clear path back to the table; the deal still generally makes sense for the parties involved, and it is likely that they will reengage at some point in the near future. Many negotiators view failure through this lens, and it does represent a good majority of failed negotiation processes. It is not uncommon for parties to reach a stalemate or deadlock and decide that a deal won't work or there is no way forward, only to come back to the table a bit later with a new idea or a different angle.

Level III: Breakdown

Level III is a more severe form of failure, where there is a lot of uncertainty about what will happen going forward. A Level III failure is characterized by a significant breakdown in the negotiation process, with the failure leading to the strong possibility that the process will not continue. It is possible for the talks to resume, but it will take a lot of work, mutual desire to restart the process, and creative thinking on both sides to make it happen. Whether this can happen depends on several factors, including the damage done to the relationship, the nature of the parties' respective BATNAs, and dynamics such as the power asymmetry between the parties, deadlines, and time pressure.

Level IV: Catastrophic Failure

Level IV failures are the most severe type. These are catastrophic scenarios where the process entirely collapses, the relationship between the parties is severely (and likely irreparably) damaged, and another effort to negotiate is highly unlikely unless something dramatic happens. This kind of failure is typically the hardest to come to grips with, because it means an almost certain end to any kind of negotiation process. Perhaps one day, after wounds heal and significant time passes, there can be another attempt at reviving talks, but not in the foreseeable future.

2

What Gets in the Way of Learning from Negotiation Failure?

The past is a place of learning, not a place of living.

—ROY T. BENNETT[1]

As you saw in the previous chapter, there are many ways to experience setbacks and to fail in negotiation, and the magnitude of those failures can be minor or major. If we accept that failure is a reality we have to face, then the next question is, when we fail, why aren't we truly learning from those failures? You might be thinking that I am making a big assumption here when I say that we aren't, but I have plenty of evidence to do so. I have had hundreds of conversations on this issue with participants in my trainings, students in my classes, and colleagues in the field, and virtually all of them suggest that we need a way to learn from these experiences and to understand what is getting in the way of our doing so.

There has been some useful work done on this question, most notably by Scott Peppet and Michael Moffitt in their article "Learning How to Learn to Negotiate."[2] Peppet and Moffitt make the case that for negotiators to truly learn from their negotiations, they need valid data about their abilities and to analyze their actual practices. They also need a willingness to engage with that information in a meaningful and thoughtful manner. The authors suggest that most negotiators don't really learn from their past experiences, due to a number of factors (including their biases and a fear of what that self-reflection might reveal).

Building on that work by Peppet and Moffitt, let me offer some specific reasons why we don't learn from our missteps and how to be conscious of these, so we don't fall into these traps. Awareness is the key that opens our eyes and then our minds.

Blame

The most dominant reason we don't learn from failure is because we are too busy engaging in the blame game and rationalizing our behavior. As any psychologist will tell you, rationalization, which is defined as "the act of finding or trying to find a logical reason to explain why somebody thinks, behaves, etc. in a way that is difficult to understand,"[3] is a powerful tool to protect one's identity. When we engage in rationalization about our own behavior, the natural progression is to blame the other or circumstances beyond our control. This takes all the fault and pressure off of us and puts it on the other negotiator, or on external circumstances. It also moves us away from an honest assessment of what transpired.

Take the example of Marvin, an entrepreneur who was negotiating with a venture capitalist (VC) named Sherice.

Marvin was seeking seed funding from Sherice to get his technology startup company off the ground. He had invested his life savings into his new company and was certain that he had a winning formula on his hands. Marvin had been cultivating a meeting with Sherice for quite some time, given her solid reputation and the connection she had to a friend of his.

As Marvin made his initial pitch to Sherice, he noticed after a few minutes that she seemed uninterested, even distracted. Becoming angrier by the second, Marvin frustratedly inquired as to whether something was wrong. Sherice looked back at Marvin and somewhat sardonically explained, "If I'm being perfectly honest, I don't quite see the value of your product. Furthermore, and perhaps more concerning from my point of view, it is not clear to me how you are differentiating yourself from the marketplace. There would need to be a lot more work put in here for me to even consider investing in this. I know that may be difficult to hear, but that is honestly where my mind is right now, since you inquired." Marvin was speechless, quietly fuming inside. He thought to himself, "How dare she, after only a few minutes of listening, tear down an idea I spent years working on! She clearly doesn't get it!" When he'd settled himself enough to speak, he angrily retorted, "You are clearly missing the importance of this product. If you don't get it from what I said, you're probably not smart enough to grasp its potential." He quickly packed up his things, stared her right in the eye, and provided one final comment, "Your loss!" as he stormed out of the room.

When Marvin got home, his wife asked how the negotiation had gone. She knew he'd had other unsuccessful negotiations with VCs in the past, and he seemed to be running out of suitors. In fact, she was getting nervous about their finances due to his lack of success. Marvin glowered at his wife and unleashed a tirade, explaining how dumb Sherice was and how he didn't want her money if she couldn't understand the value of what he was offering. Walking out of the dining room, he barked, "That woman was a moron, and she wouldn't know a good deal if it hit her in the forehead!"

Marvin was clearly not willing to look at his product and take in the criticism from Sherice in a way that might have helped him improve it. Instead, he chose to blame Sherice for the product's shortcomings and to rationalize his perspective by claiming that Sherice was intellectually incompetent and out of step with what the market wanted. Blame and rationalization are much easier for most people than taking a hard look at the criticism they receive and trying to learn from a difficult interaction—but blame in negotiation serves no purpose at all except helping us try to preserve our reputation. When we look back with a blame frame, we are focused on whose fault the failure was. Of course, this mindset prevents us from asking, "What can I learn from what just happened?" The past yields many lessons, but only if we are open to them. Blame prevents us from learning, plain and simple.

Biases and Heuristics

Another reason we do not learn from failure is the various psychological biases that we (often subconsciously) rely on to protect our image and reputation. We all have an inherent drive for self-preservation and often go to great lengths to meet this goal, whether consciously or not. There are many different biases that can help us avoid confronting our failures, which in turn helps us meet this objective. I will share just a few with you here, to give you a sense of how this works. A more comprehensive list is provided in Appendix A.

Perhaps the primary bias we need to contend with when coping with our failures is the *self-serving bias*. The self-serving bias, as defined by Elizabeth Krusemark, W. Keith Campbell, and Brett Clementz, is "any cognitive or perceptual process that is distorted by the need to maintain and enhance self-esteem, or the tendency to perceive oneself in an overly favorable manner."[4] This bias, which aids in rationalization (discussed in the previous section), pushes directly against the notion of learning from failure and leads us down various paths by which we seek to justify our actions. In negotiation, it manifests itself by the negotiator tending to ascribe success to their own abilities but to ascribe failure to factors outside their control or to the other negotiator, who they may view as unreasonable regardless of their behavior. While those attributions might well be at least partially true, and we hold certain biases for a reason, this impulse nonetheless gets in the way of us grappling honestly with our contribution to the situation and getting a holistic understanding of why the process ended in failure.

Another bias that prevents us from learning from our failures is called the *backfire effect*. This refers to the notion that when someone questions our beliefs and whether they are correct in a certain situation, we tend to dig our heels in further instead of being open to reexamining them. Suppose that two negotiators, Carl and Anita, are partway through a negotiation process. Anita objects to a piece of Carl's argument and accuses him of distorting the facts. Instead of asking Anita why she holds that perspective, Carl desperately tries to justify his facts and position. Anita continues to push back, which in turn causes Carl to get nervous and increasingly unsure of what to do. He starts spewing more facts to try to persuade her that he is correct. Anita notices Carl's defensiveness and recoils, saying she doesn't like his attitude. If he is not open to other perspectives, she states, there is not much point in continuing to negotiate. Anita packs up and abruptly leaves.

As this example suggests, a challenge with the backfire effect is that it often hinges on facts and data. This can be problematic in negotiation, because facts and data are not always what motivate people. In one study that examined misconceptions about politically charged topics as part of negotiation processes, the authors found that "giving people accurate information about these topics often causes them to believe in their original misconception more strongly, in cases where the new information contradicts their preexisting beliefs."[5] (This is related to the self-serving bias; we often don't like to admit that we might be wrong.) It follows that holding tightly to one way of trying to persuade the other negotiator—by digging in and throwing more facts at them to try to convince them that we're right—can create problems and cause us to miss signals that another approach might be more persuasive or effective.

The backfire effect is tied closely to the ego. Why is it that people tend to hold tightly to a certain position instead of letting go and recognizing that maybe there is a problem with their viewpoint, or that there might be another valid way of seeing the issue? The Enlightenment era philosopher Voltaire famously stated, "Uncertainty is an uncomfortable position. But certainty is an absurd one."[6] As a negotiator, our need to be right can have many unintended consequences—including not being open to other possibilities and missing opportunities that might appear before us in a negotiation.

As a final note here, related to biases are heuristics, which are mental shortcuts that we create to help us manage our way through life. While heuristics are very valuable tools, they also have a problem embedded within them. Many things in life look similar at first blush, but upon deeper reflection we notice they are actually quite different. To put it another way, when something looks like a duck and quacks like a duck, it might well be a duck, but upon further examination it might actually turn out to be platypus.

Allow me to provide a brief illustration of heuristics in negotiation. A common bias known as *reactive devaluation* suggests that negotiators tend to undervalue an offer from another negotiator, particularly if they hold a negative opinion of them. This bias ingrains a mental heuristic of automatic rejection without fully considering the proposal's merits. The concept of heuristics will take on additional importance later in the book, when we talk about transferring lessons from one negotiation to another.

Experience and Self-Reflection

The next reason we don't really learn from our negotiation failures is because we think experience itself is a great teacher. But is it? The answer is that experience *can* be the best teacher of all, but that requires a deep and honest analysis about what transpired in a particular negotiation. I once had a participant in a training come up to me at the end of a session to share about a negotiation situation from his past that had not gone well. After a 10-minute explanation, he finished by saying, "Some really valuable lessons in there!" I looked at him quizzically, because I hadn't really heard many great takeaways. I then inquired, "I'm curious—succinctly, what do you feel as though you really learned in the end? And how might you apply those lessons going forward?" He looked back at me with a blank stare and fumbled around for a minute trying to explain what he had learned. At that point, I invited him into a deeper conversation.

Once we'd sat down, I asked him a series of questions that got into the nuances of what he'd done and the choices he'd made. After about 30 minutes of discussion, I asked him again, "Now, tell me again, what did you learn?" He smiled at me and said, "I get it. In order to really learn the lessons, you need to do some serious soul-searching and in-depth analysis." He did get it, and I am glad he could see the difference after we had dug in a bit.

Loss Aversion

Another reason we don't learn from our failures is that we are naturally loss-averse. According to the Decision Lab, "*Loss aversion is a cognitive bias that describes why, for individuals, the pain of losing is psychologically twice as powerful as the pleasure of gaining.*"[7] Our loss aversion goes back to our ancestral past, when we were constantly having to protect ourselves from external threats. If we "lost" back then it usually meant our lives were over, so we quickly learned to turn our attention to avoiding that at all costs. That said, when we are loss-averse, we often bring to a situation a mindset that can prevent us from making the best decisions because we are desperately trying to avoid failure or risk—the fear of loss is simply too intense. This mindset can also get in the way of our learning, because we believe there was nothing else we could reasonably have done in that situation.

From a negotiation perspective, we can see that this propensity for loss aversion might cause us to pass up good opportunities, to be skeptical when it is not called for, and to be unable to recognize a failing course of action when we are engaged in one.[8] Certainly, being aware of this tendency is the first step in managing it and avoiding falling into some of the traps mentioned previously.

Lack of a Framework

The last reason we don't learn from failure that I would like to highlight is that we don't have a good framework for doing so that is not focused on blame, but rather on genuine learning. In my conversations with colleagues in the field, this has been a common refrain. When I asked them how they learned from failure, one hostage negotiator I spoke with exclaimed, "Come to think of it, we don't really have a systematic approach for doing so, but this conversation is making me think we should!"[9] I do believe many individual negotiators have their own ways of trying to learn from their failures, but there is no established or widely accepted process for this that I am aware of. If the field is going to grow, and people are going to know how and where to improve, this is crucial.

Before wrapping up this discussion, I'd like to turn to Kathryn M. Bartol, a management scholar from the University of Maryland, for an important caveat. As she stated, "When you have seen one negotiation, you have seen one negotiation."[10] Given that viewpoint, to which I subscribe to a large degree, how can a learning process be helpful for future negotiations? The answer is that any good framework should be viewed as a starting point. A worthwhile process gives the user a way forward . . . up to a certain point. It is at that juncture that the user must customize or personalize the process to suit the nuances of their specific situation, looking for commonalities while remaining aware of differences.

Self-awareness and self-reflection are the keys to learning from our failures so that we don't repeat them. As you read this chapter, I hope you thought about your own experiences and where you might have fallen victim to some of these obstacles, and how you might be able to work to avoid them in the future. Uncomfortable as this process can be, it's essential if we want to continue to grow and maximize our chances of successful outcomes in the future.

3

Overview
You Failed, Now What?

A Process for Getting Back to the Table

Don't carry your mistakes around with you.
Instead, place them under your feet and use them as
stepping stones to rise above them.

—ANONYMOUS

This chapter will provide a brief overview of the 5-step process outlined in the remainder of this book and emphasize the underlying key notion that failure offers negotiators the opportunity to learn and improve. We must go through this process while the events are fresh in our minds in order to most accurately learn from them. Procrastination is not our friend when it comes to learning from negotiations, because lessons may be forgotten or become blurred in an unhelpful manner as time passes.

Why is a process such as this so important? When we learn a new concept or idea, we tend to lack confidence in implementing it and desire a methodology to follow. I have not found a process that helps us really learn from failure, and I hope this work will fill that void in the literature and, more importantly, in our practice of negotiation. Furthermore, as we use this step-by-step approach consistently, it will become second nature. That is the ultimate goal.

To understand and recall the 5 steps in this process, it may be helpful to have an analogy to keep in mind. The analogy I propose is that of climbing a flight of stairs to get you back to the table, as depicted in Figure 3-1.

The first step in the process is accepting the reality that the negotiation did not go as planned and dealing with the loss of failing. Any time we fail, it means we did not achieve our intended goal or outcome. With that new truth comes a need to cope with the loss and what it means going forward. If we

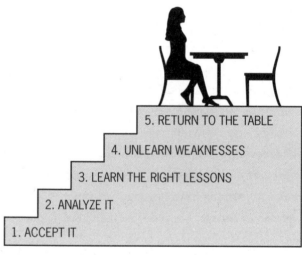

FIGURE 3-1. The 5 steps for getting back to the table

skip over this part of the process, we are not owning the disappointment and allowing ourselves to fully experience the sting of failure, so we can remember that and be motivated to not experience it again in the future.

The second step in the process is an in-depth analysis, focusing on both the Forest (the big picture) and the Trees (the minute details), to set ourselves up to truly learn from what happened and why. Too often, when we experience failure we reflect briefly, if at all, and concentrate on "moving on." But if we want to avoid repeating those failures, we must closely examine exactly what transpired and why, what we contributed, what the other party added, and what dynamics may have led us astray. If they are to be instructive for the future, we must grapple with the big-picture decisions and the minute details. This in-depth analysis enables the next step of the process.

The third element of the framework is learning the *right* lessons from a failed negotiation and how to recognize what might (and might not) be transferable to other negotiations in the future, based on the dynamics and other key dimensions. I emphasize the importance of learning the right lessons from failure because too often we attempt to apply previously learned lessons that are incorrect or unhelpful. This can reinforce poor negotiation behavior, thereby leading us down the road of further problems and mistakes. Similarly, we may try to apply lessons we've learned in the past in scenarios where they are counterproductive rather than helpful, due to differing circumstances.

The fourth step is to actively unlearn the behaviors and ideas that led us to our failure. Many of us have learned certain things about how to approach negotiation that are actually leading us astray and contributing to our weaknesses at the negotiating table. When that is the case, the most important action we can take is to purposefully unlearn those things, discarding them and making space for new ways of thinking. This may sound simple, but it requires a lot of introspection. Too often, people ignore their own weaknesses and continue to make the same mistakes over and over again.

The last step is to return to the table smarter and stronger, with a renewed sense of confidence because we know that we have improved on our weaknesses. The key in returning to the table is having better insight into who we are as negotiators, which we learn through examining our failures. To be unequivocal, no one is confident in all their negotiations or all aspects of those negotiations, but by completing the previous steps we learn the places where we are confident and become aware of those where we are not. This allows us to better prepare and to shift the balance toward the former.

Coming back to the table smarter and stronger requires a few other important aspects. The first is the *acceptance of uncertainty*, reshaping our view of that in-between cognitive state so we do not see it as so negative and frightening, and the subsequent ability to adapt to new information that is uncovered during the course of the negotiation. This skill will help us when our confidence wanes. The next is *turning our attention back* to our previous negotiation to see what we can learn from it and build upon if we are going to try to revive talks. We also have to *think through the sticking points* that caused the original failure and how we will overcome them. Finally, we must *focus on the other negotiator* and consider ways we can reengage that will be persuasive to them.

This process remains applicable even if our negotiation has truly failed—a Level IV failure with no hope of getting back to the table—although the end goal takes on a slightly different form. It is still vital to go through all of these steps, but with more of a focus on learning from them and how we might apply those lessons in our future negotiations.

The following chapters will go into depth on each of these steps in turn, laying out a process from which to learn from our failures and grow. To reiterate, this framework is intended to support us while we learn. Once we've internalized it, the steps will become second nature and form the basis of our overall learning approach into the future.

4

Step 1
You Failed—Accept It

There is no grief like the grief that does not speak.

—HENRY WADSWORTH LONGFELLOW[1]

When we experience a significant setback or fail in a negotiation, there is a process we need to undergo to deal
with what transpired effectively. That process, as Longfellow

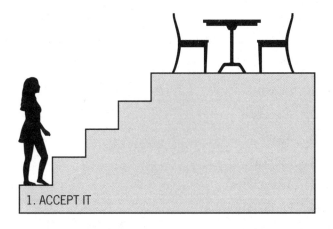

helps us to remember, begins with accepting our failure at achieving our goals and going through some form of loss acceptance or grieving. This may sound somewhat dramatic, but grief in some form—defined as the anguish experienced after a significant loss—is a critical part of the progression. If we do not grieve for what transpired, the issue or problem will remain in our consciousness, cloud our recollection of the past, and impact our vision of what is possible going forward.

In other words, we must deal with our feelings of loss, be they related to our reputation, a missed opportunity, or, in more extreme cases, something much more onerous. Many of us have learned about a model for coping with loss originally developed by psychologist Elisabeth Kübler-Ross in the late 1960s. For those who have not, the model, called the *five stages of grief*, was designed to explain how people deal with death and dying. It has since been adapted for many other realms, and, while not perfect, it does give us a point of reference to use to think about and analyze how we each individually deal with loss. From my own experience, I have seen one other important dimension take hold when learning from our negotiation failures: namely, anxiety. As such, I have added this in as an interim step between denial and anger.

According to this model, people generally grieve by going through the following stages:

1. Denial
2. Anxiety
3. Anger
4. Sadness
5. Acceptance
6. Problem solving

There is some debate about the validity of Kübler-Ross's model and whether it is accurate to say *everyone* goes through *all* these different stages. That is a fair critique, and one that I actually agree with, but the model remains a useful starting frame from which to view this challenge.[2] Importantly, we don't want to lose sight of the key point—when we fail, we must cope with that loss to truly learn from it and grow.

In Kübler-Ross's model, when we experience bad news or a significant failure of any kind, the first stage we tend to enter is denial. We often refuse to accept the new circumstances in front of us. Whether due to disbelief or the shock of not getting what we desired, denial sets in, and considering the potential implications and consequences of our failure, it's not always easy to shake off. What's more, when we hold a view of ourselves as capable and competent, it can be difficult to get past our impulse to reject or deny anything that challenges that view. To overcome denial, we must confront the truth of our situation and come to grips with our new reality.

In my experience, after some time grappling with that phase of the process, most people move on to some form of anxiety. This is because admitting we have failed also requires us to acknowledge that something did not go the way we imagined, and that we must learn more or adapt to become a more effective negotiator. There is a new truth that we are going to have to accept and manage, and we were not really prepared for that. When we truly grasp that we are not going to get what we desired, we sit in a place of great uncertainty. As such, we don't really know what to feel. Anxiousness is often the feeling we experience when there is a lack of clarity about the future. Our natural reaction when something is unsettled is an uncomfortable feeling in the pit of our stomach, and we crave some certainty to make it go away; we may find ourselves thinking, "Tell me yes or tell me no, but tell me something!"[3] We don't want to be in limbo, but until we get answers—for or against—we feel a deep unease (later in the book I will give you a different way to think about uncertainty that I hope will be helpful). For many people, our anxiety can lead to anger, because we are frustrated and don't know what else to do but get angry at the situation we are now forced to confront.[4]

When we fail, it's natural on some level to be angry about it—after all, we didn't get what we wanted or needed. When anger takes hold, we have to step back and think about why that is the case. While from a rational point of view we might want to "just let it go," our emotional selves won't allow that—not until it has been processed properly. Are we angry because we didn't meet our goals, or because our reputation or some other element of our identity has been tarnished in some way? Whatever the reason, we need to identify it and work through it. When we finally do that, we are ready to move to the next emotional level.

Sadness (expressed or unexpressed) is what typically comes next, as we recognize that we won't meet our goals or objectives. This is frequently the final step of coping before we move in a different direction; sadness indicates a certain level of acceptance about the situation, and acceptance is required in order to move on.

Finally, we come to the end of the grief cycle, where we embrace our new reality and are able to problem-solve to try to come up with a solution to help us move forward. That might mean trying to salvage the process, or thinking about what we will do in the future if reviving talks is not possible for whatever reason, or recognizing the need to grow as a negotiator and identifying the things we need to work on. It can also mean that, while keeping this new truth front and center, we have to think of new and creative ways of trying to meet at least some of our objectives differently—perhaps through our BATNA.

Interestingly, what I have seen over the years in my own work in negotiation is that people go through this process in very individual ways. Some people progress through the steps quickly, others much more slowly. Some people skip certain steps, moving right on to others. For example, some start with denial, proceed to anxiety, and then go straight to problem solving. Others, however, may go from denial to anxiety to sadness and get stuck there, without ever making it to problem solving. Some steps, it appears, are more necessary for some than others.

Some scholars who study grief have quarreled with Kübler-Ross's model, saying it is too definitive and does not account enough for individual differences. For example, in their book *Grieving Beyond Gender*, researchers Kenneth Doka and Terry Martin posit that grief is a much more complex process that is unique to the individual and has many variables, including personality and cultural background; their adaptive grief model recognizes a continuum of grieving styles.[5] It is hard to deny that individuality and cultural context play a role, on top of our common humanity, so I encourage you to take the previous discussion of the grieving process with a grain of salt and adjust it to suit your particular experience.

To bring this point about grieving to a more relatable level—particularly when it comes to building on the Kübler-Ross model and personalizing it in the way Doka and Martin suggest—let me share a story about my colleague, Stacy. I first met Stacy through our common work in the field of conflict resolution, but got to know her better when she failed in a job negotiation and reached out to me to help her understand what had happened. I went into our first conversation with Kübler-Ross's model in mind, thinking that I would watch for the curve in action—but then something curious happened. At the outset, Stacy was certainly in denial, not just about the fact that she had failed in her negotiation but about the consequences of not securing this highly coveted position. It took her some time to process her denial, but then she abruptly seemed to move on to anxiety and all the things she had planned on doing that she was not going to be able to do because she hadn't gotten the job. I could really empathize with what she was going through, but I felt my role at that point was simply to listen. I could tell it was too early to problem-solve with her and think about where she might go from this point forward.

I listened more and saw that she was really stuck in the anxiety realm. She went back and forth on a number of issues, not quite sure what to do with them or how they would affect her future plans. We had several discussions, and it took a lot of effort on my end to be patient and not try to push her forward. I could feel that I would manage a situation like hers differently, but I had to resist the urge to impose my thoughts. A week later, she called me and started uncontrollably weeping on the phone. She had entered the sadness phase and was devastated by what had happened. I tried to console her, but nothing seemed to help; I simply told her I was available if she wanted to talk. The following week I received a text from her asking if we could meet to talk about some career options. She had accepted her new reality and was ready to problem-solve.

There are two interesting takeaways from this case that speak to what Doka and Martin were referring to. The first is that Stacy never entered the anger phase. She was not the type of person that needed to experience anger to get through her disappointment about not meeting her objective. For her, it was all about sadness, which, as she explained to me when we got together, was cathartic for her and something she had likely learned from her mother after witnessing how she handled failure. She demonstrated that individuals don't necessarily need to go through each and every phase of the process—they need to do what feels natural to them. The second takeaway from this experience is the notion of pacing. I tend to be the kind of person who wants to confront a problem, deal with it, and learn from it; then I'm ready to move on to the next challenge. Stacy did not share that same mentality; she had to process things more fully before advancing to the next phase. She needed more time to experience her loss, and I needed to recognize that dynamic.

Figure 4-1 depicts the curve. As we process our failures, it's important to keep track of where we are on this curve. To do that, listen to your internal conversation.

The point of introducing this model is to highlight the importance of going through this process in a manner that works for us, given our own idiosyncrasies related to grieving and accepting failure. The idea of progressing through stages, while accounting for individual nuances and differences, is very important. Each negotiator needs to go through some process to manage their grief; the exact steps and duration may vary, but go through it they must. Otherwise, they cannot own their failure, truly learn from it, and move on.

It's worth stressing again that if we fail to grieve, in whatever way makes sense to us, we cannot progress any further—you can think of it like a backed-up sink where no water can get through. While this is a somewhat crude analogy, it's apt, because the blockage will hamper our progress until it is removed. For some, this process is easier than for others. Part of that is because of how people perceive grieving.

3. Anger
(What you might be
saying to yourself):
"I am really upset about
this. It is all their fault."

4. Sadness
(What you might be saying
to yourself):
"I am very disappointed. I am
too upset to think about dealing
with this problem."

2. Anxiety
(What you might be
saying to yourself):
"I feel uneasy and
uncomfortable. I don't
know what will happen
next."

5. Acceptance
(What you might be
saying to yourself):
"I guess this is just how
it is going to be. I need
to deal with this new
reality."

1. Denial
(What you might
be saying to yourself):
"This is not happening.
This can't be the outcome."

6. Problem Solving
(What you might be
saying to yourself):
"I know my first way of
trying to deal with this
did not work. What else
can I try?"

WHERE AM I ON THE CURVE?
Listen to the conversation in your head

FIGURE 4-1. Coping with failure

I learned a valuable lesson about grieving and my perception of it when a particular negotiation that I was involved in
did not end well. For many years, I helped to lead a non-profit
organization. As many will know, non-profits have to fundraise
from individuals and foundations. This is not an easy job, and
to make matters even more difficult, the non-profit I worked
with had a unique mission that did not neatly fall into any of the

prearranged categories that most foundations use. That made the negotiations around funding requests especially challenging.

As I prepared to meet with a foundation that I felt was perhaps the best fit for our organization, I did a lot of research and thought I had found a unique angle that would speak to them. Unfortunately, as the negotiation unfolded, I could tell my framing was not landing well despite the many different options I put in front of them. In the end, they just did not see how we fit their mission, and we did not get the money. I was frustrated and disappointed, but I did not allow myself to grieve. Rather, I immediately pushed my feelings aside and forged ahead into the next negotiation. I was determined to raise the money we needed, as I knew many people were counting on me—but I was also running away from the disappointment I knew I felt. This meant I never allowed the wounds to my ego to heal. I thought if I could succeed in my next negotiation, I could prove to myself and others that the fault did not lie with me as a negotiator, but with my counterparts, who were unreasonable and just could not understand the creative fit for their foundation. In short, I rationalized my behavior. However, because I did not really accept the loss I felt because of that failure, I unintentionally brought other issues—such as anxiety to secure the funding—into the next negotiation. Needless to say, that negotiation did not go well either, and I believe I came across as somewhat desperate. Not the best way to try to negotiate to raise money for a project!

After that second negotiation process, spurred on by comments from a close colleague, I took a few weeks to reflect before scheduling a meeting with another foundation. This time, I licked my wounds and spent time really coping with the lack of success I'd had. I allowed myself to feel bad about what had transpired and talked with the aforementioned colleague about what had happened and what I could have done differently. Once I'd done that, I found that I was able to move on to the next stage of the process and not be blocked by my own behavior. The subsequent negotiation with a different foundation a few weeks later went much differently, and I was able to finally procure the needed funding. I attribute this success to the time I took to grieve and cope properly, which readied me to manage the negotiation with a new, fresh mindset.

But how do you really accept loss? What does that mean in practice? According to one definition, acceptance in this context means embracing the moment, whether it is good or bad, in order to shape the future.[6] When you truly accept the present and the loss you've experienced, you set yourself up for the next part of the process, where an accurate analysis and understanding of what happened become essential.

5

Step 2
Analyze the Forest and the
Trees—What Went Wrong?

The only real mistake is the one
from which we learn nothing.

—HENRY FORD[1]

S omeone once told me a story about an older gentleman who
spends a few hours at a bar and becomes quite inebriated.
As he digs in his pocket after leaving the bar, he quickly realizes

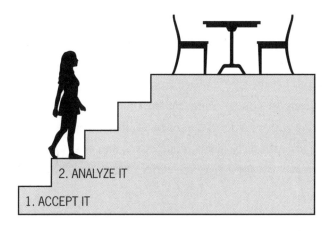

2. ANALYZE IT

1. ACCEPT IT

he has lost his keys. He frantically begins looking around the alley under the streetlight, lifting trash cans and looking under cars, making quite a ruckus. Two young men happen to be passing by at that moment and notice the man struggling. One of them asks, "Hey old man, what are you doing? Did you lose something?" The old man looks up, half his face lit by the streetlight and the other half hidden in the shadows. Slurring ever so slightly, he blurts out, "Yes, I lost my darn keys! They have to be around here somewhere." The other young man responds, "Oh, we'll help you look. Any general idea where you may have dropped them?" The old man thinks for a second, raises his wrinkled index finger, and points to the other end of the dark alley. "Most likely over there somewhere." After sharing this information, he puts his head back down and continues his search. The two young men glance at each other, smiling awkwardly, and then look back at the old man. One of them says, "Sorry, we're a bit confused. If you think you lost your keys over there [pointing down the alley], why are you digging around over here?" The old man stops and says, "Isn't it obvious? The lighting is much better here!"[2]

When I first heard this tale I laughed at the absurdity of it, but over the years in the work that I do in leadership, negotiation, and dealing with conflict I have seen this type of scenario play out far too often. When something doesn't happen as expected, we often look in comfortable (i.e., better-lit) locations as opposed to where the problem is (in the darker realms). Let me give you an example of what I mean.

Over the course of my career, I have had the pleasure of working with a number of engineering firms. Engineers are typically exceptionally smart, competent, and effective problem solvers when it comes to engineering challenges. They also tend to live most comfortably in a world of data. And therein often lies the challenge. When I work on a negotiation issue with engineers—for example, having to deal with a subcontractor's difficult project manager—they always seem to want to gravitate back to the data as the source of the problem, when that's not always what's at the heart of the issue. The challenge frequently lies elsewhere—perhaps in the underlying relationship or the unmet interests of the other party—but they're more comfortable tinkering with the data. If they carry on doing that, they will never successfully negotiate the issue because they are focusing in the wrong place. Put differently, they want to stay in the light . . . but my job is to pull them into the darkness so they can find the keys and unlock the problem. They eventually begrudgingly come along, and soon realize the value of honing in on where the problem really lies.

To genuinely understand why a failure has occurred, we must take the time to accurately analyze what happened. This analysis must happen at two levels, which I call the Forest and the Trees. The Forest is the big picture: a high-level view of the problem that allows us to gain some broad insights. The Trees are the minute details, and they help us understand what is important to take away and to potentially apply elsewhere. It is essential to go through this analytical process, or we cannot really learn what happened. It's also vital to conduct this step shortly after the negotiation concludes, so critical details can be recalled readily and most accurately. As time passes, our cognitive ability to distort what has transpired increases significantly.

In this chapter, I will walk through a series of key questions that will help us analyze what went wrong in our negotiations and why. This will include looking at the negotiation from a big-picture perspective (aka the Forest), then getting more granular and identifying critical moments as well as specific moves and turns in the process that proved to be fundamentally important (aka the Trees). I will then share a detailed negotiation example to demonstrate how this type of scrutiny works in practice.

Forest Questions

Beginning generally, we want to step back, consider the categories of failure laid out in Chapter 1, and determine which one our negotiation failure falls into and why. Take some time to carefully determine the primary issue that derailed the process, and make sure you're not just looking in the comfortable places in the light. For example, did you agree to something due to time pressure, and did it turn out to be a bad deal for you (a What Were You Thinking failure)? Or did you reach an agreement that damaged the relationship in a situation where you need the other party going forward (a Penny-Wise and Pound-Foolish failure)? From an analytical point of view, it is essential to narrow your analysis down to one of these categories. You can recognize that other types of failures may have played an exacerbating role, but for the purposes of this analysis, you need to narrow your failure down to one primary category.

Next, think about the magnitude of the failure. Was this just a temporary setback (a Level II failure), and can you think of ways of addressing the challenge and getting back to the table? Or was it a bit more severe (a Level III failure), with people's reputations being tarnished and you being left quite unsure of how to restart the process? Or, even worse, was it a negotiation earthquake (Level IV) that did irreparable damage and where restarting the process is unequivocally not going to happen?

Tree Questions

After broadly assessing what went wrong, you need to get really granular in your analysis. There are two generally related negotiation concepts that are useful to consider here: *critical moments* and *moves and turns*. I'll explain each in turn.

As explained by Michael Wheeler at a 2002 conference put on by the Program on Negotiation at Harvard Law School, critical moments are "times when significant changes occur in negotiation." Wheeler describes them as "opening moves, turning points, and tipping points," whose influence can be positive or not.[3] These moments can be macro or micro in nature, centered around significant events within the negotiation process or smaller exchanges and interactions. Here is an example of a macro critical moment.

Heather, a sales representative, had worked hard to build a relationship with Ainsley, a new potential customer. Just as the two were nearing a deal, Ainsley called Heather. "Heather, I am so sorry, but I have just been let go," she shared, with a mix of sadness and exasperation in her voice. "We have new management, and they're cleaning house. They want to bring in some of their 'own people' to the company."

"Oh, Ainsley, I am so sorry to hear that. Of course, I wish you all the best," Heather offered supportively. "Thanks," Ainsley intoned despondently. "I'll give your information to the person taking over my accounts. Take care."

A week later, Heather received a call from Jason. He introduced himself: "Heather, this is Jason. I'm taking over for Ainsley. She asked me to call you to pick up where you all left off in the negotiation." Heather, still feeling saddened, replied, "Hi Jason. Nice to meet you. I was so sorry to hear about Ainsley. We were working really well together and had the parameters of a deal ironed out. I imagine she told you about our progress."

"Yes, well, that's life," Jason retorted. "And about the deal you two had been working on—we're going to have to scrap that. It won't work for us. Frankly, I'm not sure what Ainsley was thinking. It was a terrible deal on our end. Anyway, let me put together a revised proposal that's more favorable to us, and that should still work for you. After you've read it, give me a call." And with that, Jason hung up.

Heather was beyond taken aback. Not only had Jason brushed off Ainsley's forced departure in a very insensitive manner, but he'd also thrown out what they had worked on so diligently with what seemed like very little thought or care for what Heather needed to make a deal work. Finally, from a process point of view, he didn't seem to want to engage with her, but just wanted to send over a proposal of his own without any idea of what mattered to her company.

Two days later, the proposal showed up in Heather's inbox. She really didn't feel like looking at it, so she left it for a day before opening it—and when she did, she wasn't happy with what she saw. Heather was feeling increasingly frustrated with how this process had played out. She was at the point where she didn't even want to speak to Jason, but then her phone rang. It was him. "Hi Heather, it's Jason. Did you get the revised proposal I sent? I didn't hear from you. What did you think?"

Heather took a deep breath. "Well actually Jason, this is not going to work for us. We're really far apart, and I'm uncertain where you got these numbers from and how you see this as fair—or even somewhat reasonable—to us as well. Can you explain?"

"Actually, no, I won't explain," Jason curtly replied. "This is our last and best offer. Let me know by tomorrow." And he hung up.

"The nerve," Heather thought to herself. She pulled up her email and wrote a note to Jason. The email stated, "This negotiation is over. The way in which you came in and completely disregarded all the work Ainsley and I had put in was borderline offensive. And your refusal to explain your proposal makes me think working with you going forward would not be in the best interest of me or my company. Thank you." And with that, the negotiation ended unhappily.

In this example, we see that the macro critical moment was Ainsley leaving and Jason taking over. That change completely altered the dynamic of the negotiation and the trajectory of the relationship. This was relatively easy to decipher and fits the macro critical moment category neatly.

Other macro critical moments may be less obvious at the time, with the shift being more subtle. Take the example of the married couple Joseph and Julie, who were trying to find a new home to purchase with the help of an agent named Alex. They'd been looking for some time and had even made some offers on homes, but the deals had all fallen through because Joseph and Julie kept pulling back at the last moment. Alex was getting frustrated with the fruitless negotiations and was anxious to finally make a sale. He tried his best to hide his anxiety, but it manifested in different ways.

The last home he'd taken Joseph and Julie to view really seemed to be a perfect fit for them, based on their previously articulated desires. There was very little they did not like about it. Alex thought he had finally reached the promised land of getting the two of them to make a decision. But when it came time to inspect the house, the report came back with a number of issues—one significant and the others minor. Joseph and Julie expressed some reservations given these problems, despite their expressed desire to buy the house. As they talked through the items in the report, Alex said to them, "Listen, I know this is a big decision, but we've seen a lot of houses, and this one is clearly the one you love the most. I don't think we should negotiate too hard to fix the issues in the inspection report. This is a seller's market, and you'll probably lose the house if you do." Joseph and Julie both seemed a little uncomfortable upon hearing this, but they said they would sleep on it and give him an answer in the morning.

When the morning came, Joseph called Alex and said, "We're not going through with the purchase of the house. We've also decided to find another agent—one that won't pressure us to make a sale." Alex was shocked. Indignantly, he asked what he had done to pressure them and shared a number of ways in which he felt he had been exceedingly patient with the couple. In a moment of frustration, he uttered, ". . . given your inability to make a decision." When Alex was done talking, Joseph ended the call by stating, "You just proved my point."

What happened here? And what was the critical moment? In this negotiation between the buyers and their agent, the critical moment is something we call the *intent and impact* problem. There were two instances where Alex ran into this issue without realizing it. The first critical moment was when Alex told Joseph and Julie that they should overlook the issues raised in the inspection report. While he may not have been wrong in his analysis of the market, and believed his advice was the best for them, the impact on the couple was to give them the impression that he did not care about the problems with the house—or them—and just wanted to make a sale. The second critical moment happened on the call the next morning between Joseph and Alex. When Joseph shared that they felt pressured, Alex's reply fed into the couple's narrative. Alex was trying to explain his perspective with a positive intention, but when he responded to Joseph's comment by saying they possessed an "inability to make a decision," the impact on Joseph was to confirm in his mind that he and his wife were making the right decision, and that Alex was really only interested in the sale and not their well-being. They would find someone else who would not pressure them.

The other type of critical moment is a micro one, which is often embedded in a smaller incident or exchange between the parties that is part of the larger negotiation process. However minor it may seem, that specific interchange is essential to understanding why the negotiation failed. In their book *The Shadow Negotiation*, Deborah Kolb and Judith Williams refer to this as a move or turn that a party takes in a negotiation.[4] These moves and turns can dramatically impact a negotiation in different ways, sometimes with one back-and-forth or a series of small interactions causing the whole process to fail.

There are a number of types of moves and turns in a negotiation that are made as part of a proposal or used to respond to a statement the other negotiator makes. These moves and turns include *framing, reframing, diverting, interrupting,* and *naming.* Here's an overview of each, so you can train yourself to notice them.

Framing moves are very subtle and seek to take control of the negotiation by taking the first action and shaping the conversation. Not only do those moves set the agenda, but they often do so in a manner that is unbeknownst to the other. A common example of a framing move is when an employer attempts to offer a prospective employee a package deal with a low salary because they don't have enough resources in their budget to pay the industry standard. They emphasize all the other benefits, while trying to bury the salary dimension. These moves are also designed to anchor the conversation where the framer wants it, thereby beginning a negotiation where it benefits them. A framing move can have the power to guide a negotiation toward success or failure, depending how it is done and how it is perceived by the other party (recall the earlier example of Jon Lester and the Boston Red Sox). When analyzing your negotiation failures, ask yourself: What was the initial framing of the negotiation? Who offered it? What impact did it have on the overall negotiation?

A *reframing* move takes issue with a framing move or an assertion made by the other negotiator and presents a different way of seeing the problem or challenge. If a reframing move is not made, the initial frame sets a precedent and the negotiation proceeds down that particular avenue. Let's go back to the previous scenario, where one party tries to start a salary negotiation with a lower than reasonable offer. Here, they are making a framing move and hoping you won't notice. In response to that framing move, a reframing move might sound like this: "Your offer of $60,000 for this position is really low based on my research related to industry standards. The average salary is $90,000. Can you please explain how you arrived at a figure that is two-thirds of what the salary should be?" This type of move contests the reality, or frame, the other negotiator is trying to create. Not surprisingly, such a move can create tensions and possibly lead the process down a difficult path toward failure. Ask yourself, did I make a reframing move, and was it that move that failed? What impact did that move have on the process? Or, if there were reframing moves that could have been taken but you missed an opportunity to do so, might that have led to the failure?

A *diverting* move seeks to redirect and, to some extent, depersonalize the conversation by focusing on the substance of the problem. Carrying on with our example, rather than making a reframing move by challenging the lowball offer, you could nudge the negotiation toward your qualifications and the value you bring to the position. This way, you may be able to avoid the sort of haggling that might get you stuck. A diverting move can be helpful in a number of ways, but it can also result in you getting bogged down in another issue or cause you to fail to address the issue on the table at the moment. In the end, that could lead to larger problems in a negotiation. Ask yourself, did I make a diverting move, and what impact did it have? Was it what I intended or was it perceived differently? Reflecting back on the negotiation, were there diverting moves that you could have taken that might have helped to avoid failure?

The next kind of move that's commonly found in negotiations is an *interrupting* one. A short break, or reconvening the next day, can change the dynamic and flow of an unproductive process and help to reset the negotiation. In our example, you might decide to take a brief coffee break to think about what to do next. Be aware, though, that while these are perfectly reasonable moves in negotiation, such breaks can sometimes prove to be micro critical moments and carry different meanings. If such a move were suggested in a sales negotiation, for example, it would likely be viewed differently. As a friend who has been in sales for many years once shared with me, "If I don't close a deal then and there, and someone wants to get back to me, that usually means I'm going to lose the deal. So, I do everything to try to keep them from walking out the door—even for a few minutes."[5] The varying possible readings of this type of move can lead to misinterpretations and misunderstandings, so be as clear as possible as to why you are taking it. In your analysis, ask yourself if a break could have helped head off an escalatory cycle, and if so, where. Alternatively, might taking a break have sent the wrong signal and led to further issues in the process?

Finally, there is the move of *naming*, which is outwardly labeling a tactic or overall approach being used in a negotiation. This move points out to the other negotiator that you are aware of what is going on and what they are trying to do.[6] In our salary negotiation example, you could have said, "Based on my research on industry standards for this position, your offer seems quite low. Unless you can give me a good explanation as to why this makes sense, I'm not certain there is much to negotiate." This is a much more direct statement than the reframing move described earlier. Naming moves may have two possible impacts. On the one hand, naming something can lead to further issues and an escalation, particularly if your naming of what the other party is doing is incorrect. On the other hand, letting the other person know that you understand what they are doing may help them to realize their tactic will not work, and they may seek to change course. This has to be done with a great deal of thought and tact. Such a move has to be managed carefully, or it could send the negotiation down the wrong road. If you named something in your negotiation in an effort to point out that you understood what was happening, what was the impact? If it was negative, could you have done it in a different manner so it had a better effect?

Hopefully, these examples have given you an idea of how to identify critical moments and important moves and turns in your own negotiations and how they can help you understand the outcome. In the case of a macro critical moment, like the changing of negotiators from Ainsley to Jason, what might you have done differently to stop the process from collapsing? With a micro critical moment like the initial low salary offer, what interaction was the one that doomed the process, and what other possible moves were at your disposal?

This type of examination is extremely helpful in theory, but to really understand how to do it, the best approach is to apply it to one of your own negotiation failures. The following worksheet (Figure 5-1) will walk you through the sequence of the analysis, beginning with getting a Forest perspective on the type and magnitude of your failure. After that, you can begin to consider the Trees by getting a bit more detailed in your assessment: Review the actions you took that contributed to the failure, the dynamics involved that hindered progress, the information that was hidden that you have since come to understand, the role of the other negotiator, and the aforementioned macro and micro critical moments. All of this will help you understand what happened and why, what you could have done differently, and whether the process can be salvaged at this juncture.

Now that you have had a chance to assess why you failed from a Forest and Trees perspective, it is essential that you learn from what occurred and carry that forward. This requires careful scrutiny of your analysis, going beyond the obvious lessons to make sure that the ones you take away are the correct ones and that you know when to apply those lessons elsewhere (and when not to, because the lessons might not fit due to the differing dynamics and circumstances).

What Went Wrong Worksheet

Name of the Negotiation:

_____

Forest Questions

Generally, what are the reasons for the failure in this negotiation? Think back to the 7 different types of failure. Which one fits best and why?

_____
_____
_____
_____
_____

What level of failure is this? If it is a I, II, or III, what can you do to resurrect the process?

_____
_____
_____
_____
_____

Tree Questions

Gradually move from the general and broad to the narrow and granular. Take each element listed above and dissect it further below:

1) What did you contribute to the failure and what, if anything, could you have done differently?

_____
_____
_____
_____

2) What dynamics were involved that you did not handle well or failed to notice that contributed to the failure?

_____
_____
_____

3) What information was hidden from you at the beginning, or during the process, that aided in the failed negotiation?

_____

_____

_____

4) What role did the other negotiator play in the failed process?

_____

_____

_____

5) Can you pinpoint a critical moment (macro) or specific move or turn (micro) in the negotiation that was pivotal to the failed outcome?

_____

_____

_____

FIGURE 5-1. Determining what went wrong

6

Step 3
Not Just Any Lessons—
Learn the Right Ones

Experience is not the best teacher, evaluated experience is.

—JOHN C. MAXWELL[1]

The previous learning step—conducting a big-picture and granular analysis—was designed with a very specific goal in mind. A classic mistake that we make as negotiators is not taking

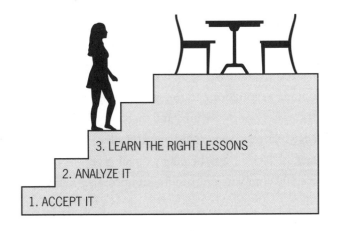

3. LEARN THE RIGHT LESSONS

2. ANALYZE IT

1. ACCEPT IT

the time to learn from our failures. But even when we do, often the lessons we try to transfer aren't actually applicable to our new negotiations, whether because of differences in the contexts and dynamics or because, as discussed in Chapter 2, our unconscious biases and heuristics lead us to learn the wrong ones. If we don't learn the right lessons, we may both develop a false sense of security and apply those lessons incorrectly in our future negotiations. As a result, we are likely to repeat the mistakes that really caused the failure in the first place. "I'll never do that again . . ." is a common refrain, but one that often leads us astray.

Applying the lessons we've learned, and making sure they're the correct ones, is tricky business. This is because, again using the words of Kathyrn Bartol, "When you have seen one negotiation, you have seen one negotiation." Of course, what Bartol is getting at is that each negotiation has its unique dimensions, and no two negotiations are ever *exactly* the same. However, many negotiations do share a number of similarities, and there are lessons that can be drawn from one and applied to another if this is done thoughtfully and with great care. That is what I aim to show you in this chapter.

The transferring of lessons learned happens at two levels. The first level is behaviors, in the form of tactics and skills. These are the easiest to correct and work with. The second level is attitudes, in the form of a negotiator's mindset and underlying beliefs. These are influenced by what we have learned and internalized in the past, as well as the experiences that have defined our negotiations to this point in our lives. Let's start with the easier one, behaviors, and then we will move on to the challenge related to our underlying attitudes.

Back in 2022, I was helping a small group of people at a Fortune 500 company prepare for an upcoming negotiation. A woman named Talia asked me if she could talk to me at lunch about a negotiation she'd been involved in that had not gone very well, and to get my advice about that experience and how to use it to prepare for an upcoming negotiation. When we sat down, Talia explained to me that she had been part of a team of three people tasked to negotiate with a prospective client on behalf of her company. The negotiation was designed to secure work from the client, with each negotiator having a different role and bringing a certain skill set to the table: one person was in sales, the other a legal expert, and Talia was the subject matter expert. Talia recounted how the team had met and all believed they were aligned going into the negotiation . . . and then everything fell apart. It turned out they were not unified on some key issues, including their bottom line, the acceptable length for the contract, and levels of risk. These internal divisions caused them much embarrassment and frustration, and ultimately led to a collapse of the process. She ended her initial explanation by exclaiming, "So many valuable lessons that I can take into this upcoming negotiation!" I asked her if she could give me more details about that negotiation, so I could understand the parallels. As she explained further, the two scenarios seemed very different to me.

As Talia began to summarize the lessons she'd learned from the previous negotiation that she planned to apply, I pointed out the unique nature of this upcoming negotiation and commented that she should be careful about transferring those past lessons to this one. This seemed to both confuse and intrigue her, so I pointed out some distinct and critically important dynamics from the previous negotiation that did not appear to exist in the upcoming one. These differences meant that trying to transfer her learnings could lead to tactical mistakes. For example, there were different numbers of people on the two negotiation teams; in the first negotiation her team had made the first offer, while in the upcoming negotiation it did not seem to make sense to do so; there was a power symmetry in the first negotiation but not in the upcoming one; and there had been diverse negotiation styles within her team in the previous negotiation, whereas it didn't sound like that would be the case in the future scenario. She began to understand what I was getting at and why I was cautioning her to be careful. By the end of our conversation, Talia had realized that many of the lessons she had intended to bring to this negotiation were actually not really applicable. She told me she was glad we had talked the issue through at some length, so she wouldn't make a mistake by attempting to put them to use incorrectly.

What I was talking about with Talia was really behaviors and tactics; actions we take in the room. However, there is a deeper level at play in negotiation, in the form of our underlying mindset and attitudes, and we need to analyze these too and be prepared to learn and adapt. To this end, it's useful to consider a concept called *transference*, which is grounded in psychodynamic theory. Simply put, transference is the idea of using old patterns of thought and action to organize and give meaning to present experiences.[2] Being aware of transference can aid us by reminding us to look for ideas and beliefs that are rooted in our psyches and deeply held, without us realizing it.[3]

So how does transference work in negotiation? Let me provide you with a few examples so you can begin to become familiar with this issue and how it can manifest in these processes. First, consider the case of Ronnie. Early in Ronnie's career, he engaged in many negotiations with his boss, Harold, and to put it kindly, they did not go well. Harold was an old-school, hard-nosed negotiator who saw everyone—including Ronnie—as an adversary. As a result, Ronnie rarely got what he was seeking, and he left those interactions feeling defeated. Furthermore, Ronnie came away with a very jaded, hardened perspective on negotiation. It felt uncomfortable to him, but he believed this manipulative, win/lose approach was the way you negotiated to be successful.

Eventually, Ronnie moved from an internally focused job to an external sales role. Harold worked hard with Ronnie to prepare him for this new position. Ronnie began to take a very tough approach to his sales negotiations, manipulating others and taking advantage whenever possible. Harold was pleased with Ronnie's approach and the successful results he shared. Ronnie was able to make a number of initial sales, but he noticed he didn't have many repeat customers. Harold told him that was okay, and the nature of negotiation. This arrangement came to a screeching halt a year later when Harold became ill and had to retire.

A new CEO, Rosa, took over, and she had a diametrically opposed approach to negotiation compared to Harold. Rosa's negotiation approach was about seeking mutual gain and investing in long-term relationships with clients. Her philosophy could be summed up as, "Your current customer is your best future customer if you treat them right and respect the relationship."

Shortly after Rosa took the helm, Ronnie engaged in a negotiation where he was very hard on an existing customer that had recently been transferred to him after another salesperson left the company. Immediately afterward, Rosa received a call from the long-standing client, who, clearly angry, asked her if she was aware of Ronnie's manipulative tactics. The representative explained that they were not interested in this kind of working relationship and were prepared to go elsewhere should this approach continue. Rosa inquired further and was taken aback by what she heard. She immediately called Ronnie in to her office and told him about the call she'd just received. Ronnie was surprised and replied, "But I got a good deal, and this is how I sell. It's how Harold taught me to negotiate." Rosa glared at him. "Well, in the short term, yes, but you jeopardized the long-standing relationship. That is not how we do things anymore at this company, and it's high time you learned the value of these relationships. They are the lifeblood of everything we do. This conversation is not over. In fact, this is just the beginning." Ronnie's head dropped. As he stared at the floor, he felt a mixture of anger and confusion.

When he left Rosa's office, Ronnie genuinely wondered where the problem was. After all, he'd simply done what he'd been taught to do, and Harold had always been happy with his work. So what was he doing wrong? He began to reach out to other salespeople that Rosa had recently brought into the company, and he learned that they took an entirely different approach to negotiation. He knew that, given Rosa's focus, if he wanted to have a future at the company he needed to change his perspective and learn this new approach.

Ronnie had fallen victim to a mindset issue, which was coupled with deeply ingrained transference through Harold's humiliation of him at the negotiating table. He had learned how to use an approach to negotiation that might work in the short term and in one-time negotiations, but that certainly creates problems in the longer term by damaging important relationships. Ronnie never understood the downside of the one-sided, win/lose approach because Harold never explained it to him; he was adamant that this was how you negotiate.

Once Ronnie had internalized Harold's approach, he subconsciously applied it to all his negotiations, regardless of the situation; he was driven to assert his own dominance and "win" at all costs. Only after Rosa confronted him did he realize that the approach he had been taking was self-defeating behavior as a salesman, since it led to him not having many repeat customers. He now recognized that he needed to stop transferring this approach to all his negotiations and learn a new way of negotiating.

In a case like Ronnie's, where applying the process we've used to solve an earlier problem makes later problems harder to solve, we call this *negative* transference. In effect, we have taken an incorrect approach to that initial challenge, not realized it, and sought to apply it in a future situation where it has little chance of succeeding. Let me share another negotiation situation to help reinforce this point.

Aylee was in a very difficult spot. Time was running out for her and Cassie to make a deal. Aylee had made about as many concessions as she could from a financial perspective; anything more, and an agreement really did not make sense for her company. But she and Cassie were still $250,000 apart. Aylee thought long and hard about whether she should let go of the deal, but in a last-ditch effort to save it, she offered a way forward. She would accept $125,000 less on the two-year deal, but Cassie had to commit in writing that her company would renegotiate more favorable terms the next time around, when the deal expired. Cassie quickly agreed. When Aylee came back to her boss, she lauded her for her ability to get the deal done. Aylee expressed some doubts related to the final agreement, but her boss affirmed her actions by saying, "Hey, that's how negotiations go." Aylee felt better about the situation and what she had done. This type of give and take, she thought to herself, was a good thing, and the key to making negotiations work.

Fast-forward six months, and Aylee was engaged in another negotiation with a potential client named Jesse. Jesse was driving a hard bargain; the terms that were proposed were much less favorable than in the previous negotiations Aylee had engaged in. In addition, he was acting quite difficult—which did not bode well for the future, since she knew she would have to work with him to implement the deal and troubleshoot issues over the course of the contract. As Aylee weighed her options, she remembered her prior last-minute compromise, and her boss's words—"Hey, that's how negotiations go"—kept reverberating in her head. Jesse pressed her impatiently: "I need an answer!" Aylee took a deep breath and agreed. Jesse slyly smiled.

Aylee left not feeling great about the agreement, but she was comforted by the feeling that her boss would support her decision, as she had done in the previous negotiation. When they met, Aylee explained the deal and what she'd agreed to. Her words were greeted with a look of shock and dismay. "Why," her boss implored, "would you agree to those terms? What were you thinking?" With a sinking feeling, Aylee tried to justify what she had done and finished by requoting her boss's statement about the nature of negotiation. She looked at Aylee quizzically and said, "Yes, that agreement made sense in the last deal. Not in this one. The first negotiation was with a long-standing customer who we were fairly certain, based on their previous actions and the contract they signed, would provide business in the future and who had proven they were easy to work with and stood by their word. The second negotiation was with a new customer, you mentioned they seemed difficult, and we have no idea how this relationship will turn out. Didn't you understand those key differences?" Aylee left the room feeling embarrassed and a little ashamed.

What can we take away from this story? The two negotiations seemed analogous to Aylee, and she did not understand why her approach was acceptable in one and not the other until after the fact. When she was pressed to make a decision, she fell back on applying the same thinking and mindset from the first negotiation to the second, without really considering the differences between the two. This is a trap all of us have probably fallen into at some point. How, then, do we ensure that we only transfer the correct lessons from one negotiation to the next?

We can begin by recognizing the telltale signs that negative transference may be occurring. According to mental health writer Stephanie Harrison, one clear sign of (negative) transference is "when your feelings or reactions seem bigger than they should be. You don't just feel frustrated, you feel enraged. You don't just feel hurt, you feel deeply wounded in a way that confirms your most painful beliefs."[4] In other words, our deeply held feelings about one situation are clearly, and perhaps disproportionately, impacting our approach. This is typically a subconscious process. Thus, a key aspect of dealing with this challenge is bringing those underlying thoughts and beliefs into the conscious realm so we can manage them.

It is also vital that we analyze our negotiations for comparability, which builds on the Forest and Trees analysis in the previous step. The following questions can help you understand the places where the biggest differences between negotiations can be seen (an explanation as to why follows each question). Notice the mix of tactical, or skills-based, challenges along with behavioral and mindset ones. There will be more on the latter in the next step in our process as well.

When comparing two negotiations, ask yourself:

- Did they involve the same number of parties?

    If there are two parties in one negotiation and many more in the other, the processes will be very different. Two parties have one set of dynamics; more parties add more layers and complexity.

- Was one negotiation focused on a single issue, whereas in the other there were multiple topics to work through?

    Single-issue negotiations are often approached in one way, while multiple-issue negotiations require numerous process choices. For example, in multi-issue negotiations the subjects under discussion may be dealt with one at a time, or woven together in a package, or a trade-off approach can be taken based on the parties' respective valuations.

- Was one negotiation focused only on the short term, where the relationship did not matter (i.e., a one-time encounter), while the other had both a short- and a long-term dimension (i.e., there will be further negotiations in the future)?

    In short-term negotiations the relationship is not so critical, so you can negotiate with that in mind. In long-term negotiations the short term matters, but equally important is the relationship that is built over time.

- Are there subtle similarities between the current negotiation and a previous one that did not go well that might be causing negative transference?

There might be things about the other negotiator or the situation itself that remind you (even subconsciously) of past experiences, and these negative associations might be getting in the way of your approach. Your counterpart might look, sound, or act similarly to someone you've dealt with in the past, or there might be similarities in the circumstances—for example, if you're facing a significant power disparity.

- Were the negotiation styles used by the parties involved the same or different?

   The Thomas-Kilmann model describes five conflict handling modes, or styles, that are commonly encountered in negotiation: competing, accommodating, avoiding, collaborating, and compromising.[5] It can be useful to keep these in mind in your negotiations, and perhaps adapt your own style based on that of your counterpart. If you are negotiating with a person who has a competing style, for example, you will probably want to take a different approach than if you are dealing with an accommodator, adapting your message and tone to the situation at hand. If you were dealing with different styles from the first negotiation to the second, that is also something to consider and weigh the impact of.

- Were the dynamics in the negotiations the same or different?

   Here are some prominent dynamics that you will want to consider:

   - Was there trust in one negotiation, but mistrust (or unfamiliarity) in another?

- Were the power differentials between the parties distinct from one negotiation to the next? (I.e., was there a power symmetry in one negotiation and an asymmetry in the other?)
- Were the negotiators of the same gender? If not, what impact might that have?
- Were all the negotiators from a single culture in one negotiation and from different cultures in another negotiation?
- Were there generational differences in one negotiation and not the other (or different generational disparities in each)?
- Were there time pressures or deadlines in one negotiation and not in the other?

The bottom line when it comes to learning and transferring the right lessons is comparability and understanding when our approach to negotiation and underlying mindset might be leading us awry. A negotiator must learn to recognize which negotiations are similar enough and have enough of the same dynamics that lessons learned from past experiences can appropriately be applied. Conversely, in negotiations that are dissimilar, we need to pay attention to those unique features and think carefully about which lessons are applicable and which are not. Once we are as certain as we can be that we've learned the right lessons from our experience, we can move on to the next step of identifying our weaknesses and actively unlearning the thoughts and behaviors that caused our challenges or failures in the first place.

7

Step 4
Actively Unlearn What Your Weaknesses Taught You

If you always do what you have always done, you will always get what you have always gotten.

—JANE KIRKPATRICK[1]

We all have a story about ourselves as a negotiator that we have built up over the years based on our accumulated knowledge and experience. That's how human beings work.

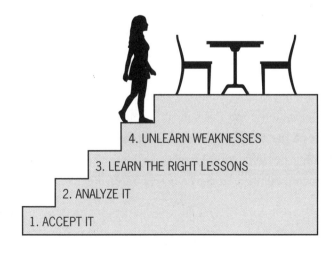

4. UNLEARN WEAKNESSES

3. LEARN THE RIGHT LESSONS

2. ANALYZE IT

1. ACCEPT IT

While this somewhat idealized self-image may help us when it comes to our negotiations, there may also be a downside to it. As we know, setbacks and failures at the negotiation table can occur for many reasons. Some are in our control and others are not. Much of the time, failures can be traced back to a negotiator's weaknesses, or those aspects of negotiation with which we struggle. It follows, then, that if we educate ourselves about our weaknesses, and remain open to challenging our current stories of who we are as negotiators, we give ourselves the best chance to minimize our mistakes and failures in the future.

If we are going to learn from our mistakes and improve on our weaknesses, we need to look not only outward but also inward. As you have probably noticed, the steps we've taken up to this point have involved a mix of both, but now we're going to shift our attention more fully to introspection. This can be uncomfortable, but we cannot improve as negotiators without self-reflection.

Some of our weaknesses as negotiators will come from what we have learned is the right way to negotiate.[2] Unfortunately, many things that people learn about negotiation from different sources get in the way of them becoming more effective negotiators (for example, in the case of Robbie, described in the previous chapter, an adversarial mindset and taking a short-term, win/lose approach). The strategy that I am advocating in this step is to actively *unlearn* the things that are getting in our way and blocking us from progressing. We will start there and then come back around to more on how to learn from our weaknesses.

As we delve into this subject, I want to explain the importance of the word *active* when it comes to unlearning. It is certainly possible to unlearn something by accident or in a haphazard manner. However, active unlearning means that we consciously recognize a problem with an idea or behavior and purposefully seek to change it.

To help with active unlearning of problematic negotiation behaviors and ways of thinking, I have created a chart that you can fill in to, somewhat objectively, come to grips with your weaknesses. The chart, shown in Figure 7-1, has three columns: one where you list what you see as your weaknesses, one where you explain why you think you have each of those weaknesses (i.e., how you learned that aspect of negotiation), and one where you describe what you need to unlearn in order to improve or change.

Figure 7-2 shows an example of what this might look like, so you can get a better sense of how it works in practice.

When it comes to weaknesses in negotiation, it's important to start from the premise that we all have them. As you consider your own weaknesses, think more generally about your problem areas, and try to contemplate what role each of them might have played in a negotiation where you had a very negative setback or failed. How might they have led you to make the wrong moves or decisions?

Weaknesses, Why You Hold Them, and What to Unlearn

My weaknesses	Why I have them	What do I need to unlearn?
1.	1.	1.
2.	2.	2.
3.	3.	3.
4.	4.	4.
5.	5.	5.

FIGURE 7-1. Weakness chart

Weaknesses, Why You Hold Them, and What to Unlearn

My weaknesses	Why I have them	What do I need to unlearn?
1. Seeing the other negotiator as an adversary.	1. I learned that I have to gain as much as I can in the short term and to deal with the longer term later.	1. That short-term success is all that matters and I don't need to worry about nurturing long-term relationships.
2. Viewing compromise as synonymous with negotiation.	2. I was taught you have to give something up of great importance in negotiation to reach an agreement.	2. That compromise is a core aspect of all negotiations—I don't always have to give something up that is important to me to meet my objectives.
3. Learning that I have to keep emotions out of negotiation.	3. I have seen many negotiations fall apart because people's emotions got the better of them.	3. That emotions only have a destructive impact on negotiation and they can actually be kept out of the process.

FIGURE 7-2. Weakness chart with examples

Some of your weaknesses might be conscious and others subconscious. With the latter, we often have to really dig deep to uncover them. It might be helpful to talk with a friend or colleague and get their external perspective on your negotiation abilities. Often, other people see things we do not and can help us reflect on them in a productive manner.

After listing our weaknesses, we must ask ourselves why those weaknesses exist. How did we develop them, and what will we need to do to change those attitudes and behaviors? That exploration will naturally lead us to a question that is critically important at this juncture: How can we actively unlearn the behaviors that have led us astray and change our mindset to something more productive?

Let me give an example of how to do this, before we go further into active unlearning. A common weakness for many of us is not being assertive enough in negotiation.[3] That is the action to work on. Next, ask yourself, "Why do I struggle to be assertive?" One answer might be that society tells certain groups of people, which you may be part of, that it is not appropriate for them to assert their needs. This view may be bolstered by the notion that they should be grateful for what they have and just take what the other negotiator offers. This can lead them to associate assertiveness with being greedy, or to feel that they are unworthy of asking for what is important to them. It's important to be honest with yourself, however uncomfortable it might be, and to acknowledge those often deeply ingrained, subconscious thoughts and feelings. Once you have done this, ask yourself, "*What do I need to unlearn* so I don't get led astray in the future?" If you somehow have come to associate assertiveness with being greedy or feel that you are not worthy of asking for what you want, you need to unlearn that narrative and replace it with a new story. The new story is that to be an effective negotiator you must be assertive and push for what you need in a negotiation, or you will never receive it. Remember, *if you never ask in negotiation, you will always know the answer*. The process is as simple as that, although pinpointing why we engage in certain behaviors is not as easy as it sounds and may require some significant contemplation. Notice as well that what you need to unlearn is often more complex and goes deeper than the weakness itself.

The famous management theorist Peter Drucker once said, "If you want to start doing something new, you have to stop doing something old."[4] Actively unlearning creates the necessary space to do something new and different. Add to this reality psychologist Herbet Gerjuoy's observation, "The illiterate of the 21st century will not be those who cannot read and write, but those who cannot learn, unlearn, and relearn."[5] So, if we accept the importance of unlearning as a truism, how exactly do we go about unlearning knowledge and behavior that have guided us for so long?

To understand how to unlearn, we must define what it means to do so. Unlearning is more than simply forgetting what we know. It's a deliberate process that we undertake to scrutinize and purge our unhelpful beliefs and habits. In our case, unlearning means examining and challenging old negotiation ideas and principles that are getting in the way of new learning. Consider again the example of Ronnie, whose former boss, Harold, had instilled in him a belief that negotiation was all about domination and winning. For Ronnie to change and improve as a negotiator he had to become aware of this problem, as Rosa helped him to do, and then consciously unlearn what he thought was the proper way to negotiate.

To unlearn, we must begin by becoming aware of how our behavior is problematic, then question and challenge the assumptions we make, biases we hold, and underlying attitudes we possess that contribute to our thought processes and mindset. This can be a much more difficult process than most realize, because that mindset is comfortable, familiar, and deeply embedded in our practices. Think about the analogy of visiting a different country with a very distinct culture from your own. Many people struggle with this challenge and find the process of acclimating to another culture disorienting and confusing. This experience, known as "culture shock," can sometimes occur in the realm of negotiation as well, because we may find that what we've learned from our own past experiences about ways of interacting no longer apply in a different setting. We have to unlearn those ways of thinking and acting and learn completely new patterns if we are to make sense of our new surroundings and operate effectively in that context.

Here's an example from my own experience. For many years I have worked on a project called the Abraham Path, a long-distance walking and traveling route across the Middle East with the goal of connecting people from outside the region to people inside it in a unique manner. My travels have taken me to many places, including Southeast Turkey, where I spent time in the famous town of Harran in Şanliurfa Province. This area could not have been more different culturally from the one I grew up in. The culture in that part of Turkey is what is often called an *honor culture*, which is "characterized by a complex set of beliefs, attitudes, and norms about the importance of personal reputation, and the necessity of protecting and defending one's reputation and social image" and where "people have richer conceptions of the concept of *honor*, and they perceive that more situations are imbued with honor-related implications."[6] When I first began to work with the local communities, many of whom lived in a feudal system with chieftains (known as Agas), I failed to fully grasp their way of seeing the world. Eventually, I realized my way of seeing and understanding the world simply did not apply in that setting. I had to put my Western perspective aside, unlearn the values that underpinned my culture in the short term, and learn what it really meant to live in this type of culture so that I could speak to what would be most important to them. It was not easy, and I failed in different ways until I finally figured it out and achieved success in the long term.

Thus, when it comes to unlearning, we may actually have to acknowledge that the habits that we have developed were never as effective as we believed. That will liberate us to eliminate ideas and beliefs that no longer help us, or that actually hold us back. Let's take one concept that I think every negotiator needs to unlearn in order to excel—namely, that compromise is an essential part of negotiation.

Why do we need to unlearn this idea to be an effective negotiator? Many of you reading this may find that notion shocking, thinking that compromise forms the core, or at least a very big part, of your overall negotiation strategy. However, this mindset can hold you back in unexpected ways.[7] Let me explain. It is my contention that going into a negotiation with the expectation that you will need to compromise focuses your energy and attention on what you have to give up to get where you want to go. People often revert to compromise before they actually know the challenge they are dealing with or the real underlying interests of the other party. Do you really think it is prudent to give up something of significant importance to you before you even know if you must? I don't believe it is. In fact, I have often stated that compromise should be the very last stop in someone's decision making in negotiation, not the first.[8]

Compromise is about reaching an expedient solution and moving on to the next problem or challenge. In negotiations where time is of the essence this might be preferred, but when that is not the case, do we really want our very important negotiations focused on expediency instead of reaching the best solution possible? To put this into context, think about negotiated solutions from history related to compromise. An example that springs to mind is the Three-Fifths Compromise, where it was agreed that three-fifths of slaves would be counted toward a Southern state's total population—or put another way, Black Americans were counted as three-fifths of a White American. Similar legislated deals included the Missouri Compromise and the Compromise of 1850. Going back further in history, how about King Solomon's compromise solution to cut the baby in half? Thankfully, the real mother stepped forward, but imagine if she had not! The alternative to compromise is creative problem solving, where we seek to understand the problem and the underlying interests of the parties involved so we can maximize all the value that can be had in a negotiation. We seek the best solution, not just the most obvious or quickest one. I prefer the maximizing approach, as I think most would, if they really thought about it carefully.

Through my work, training, and teaching, I have also found that compromise has another important downside. Subconsciously, compromise pushes people to dislike, or even loathe, the process of negotiation. As some people have stated to me, "Who wants to engage in an important process over something meaningful when the only way to reach an agreement is to give up something very important to them?" I don't know too many people who would be tempted by that prospect. This perspective is very unfortunate for the field, and one I hope will be challenged by this and other analyses.

Hopefully, these points have helped clarify my earlier assertion that compromise is something negotiators need to unlearn, replacing it with problem solving and creative thinking. By focusing our attention on problem solving we make certain that we are addressing the heart of the issue, exploring our own and the other party's interests, and engaging in an inventive process to meet those interests in the best way possible. That formula has proven to be far more effective for me over the years than reverting to less-than-optimal compromise arrangements.

Once we recognize the importance of actively unlearning unproductive behaviors and ways of thinking, we need a model to follow that will help with this often arduous task. The components of the model I use, originally developed by the organization Fearless Design and built on by me, are *awareness, unlearning, relearning, habit forming, practice*, and *unlearning again* (see Figure 7-3). The concept I added to the original model is awareness. The reason I did so is that understanding that there is a problem with our current thinking is a vital first step. If we don't see the problem in our thinking, we won't understand the need to actively unlearn our current beliefs and behaviors and engage in the difficult work it takes to do so.

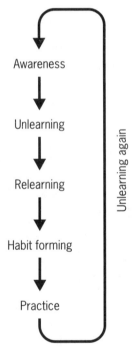

FIGURE 7-3. The unlearning cycle[9]

After realizing there is a problem with our current thinking, the first part of the process is to take steps to actively unlearn what is getting in the way of our success. This requires some contemplation of what the problem is and why we need to learn something new (recall our earlier conversation about lacking assertiveness). Being clear about this is essential, because we definitely don't want to unlearn something that is useful.

Once we have gotten rid of those obstacles, we must engage in the relearning of new information and ways of thinking and acting that will help us meet our needs and goals more effectively. With repetition, we can ensure that these become deeply embedded, forming new habits that we can then put into practice in our negotiations. This process will absolutely be helpful, but we must also remain open to the possibility that at some point we may recognize other problem areas, or our new learning may run into its own problems, and we may have to revisit that as well. That is when we start the unlearning process all over again. As you can see, this is a cyclical journey that we should be prepared to repeat over time.

I hope by now I've established the importance of unlearning the thoughts and behaviors that lead to our failures in negotiation, but you might still be struggling with identifying them. To give you a starting point, the following sections outline some of the concepts and beliefs that guide many negotiators and often lead them to failure. Many of these are more traditional outlooks that have become somewhat outdated and been replaced with newer methodologies and ways of thinking, but it's still very common to come across them. To be fair, they may all be valid and applicable in certain specific circumstances, but more often than not these are ideas and mindsets that we should unlearn. When we find ourselves espousing them in our negotiations, we must ask ourselves if they are guiding us in the right direction, and whether they are helping us or leading us astray.

Compromise

I've already talked quite a bit about compromise, but I wanted to share one more example. In their classic book *Getting to Yes*, Roger Fisher, William Ury, and Bruce Patton tell the story of two people who are studying in a library: one person wants a window open and the other wants it closed.[10] A compromise solution might be to close the window part of the way, not really satisfying either party. As the two people continue to argue, their tone getting louder and louder, a librarian comes over to quiet them and to try to determine what is going on. She begins by asking each person *why* they want the window open or closed. The person who wants the window open explains that they want some fresh air because they are getting sleepy. The other person, who wants the window closed, explains that the breeze is blowing their papers around. The librarian thinks for a moment, walks to the next aisle, and opens that window. With that solution, fresh air comes in but is not directly blowing the papers everywhere. Problem solved, no compromise needed. The takeaway? Rather than assuming that you will need to give up something you want to reach an agreement, replace that thinking with the following analysis:

1. What don't I know about the situation?
2. What is motiving me? What are the things I value/care about in this negotiation?
3. What do I know about what is motivating the other negotiator? Do I really know what they value/care about?

This series of questions helps us unlearn the impulse to compromise and focus instead on grasping the underlying interests involved and what people truly value. This, in turn, more easily leads to effective problem solving.

Keep Emotions Out of Negotiation

Another concept that many of us have to unlearn is that we must keep emotions out of negotiation. Why? Well, human beings are by nature both logical and emotional creatures. As such, it is impossible to keep emotions out of negotiation.[11] The effort we put in to try to do this—usually by attempting to suppress them—often makes things worse, because those emotions exist, whether they are openly expressed or not. In fact, there is ample evidence, laid out notably by Roger Fisher and Daniel Shapiro, that shows that suppressing emotions instead of expressing them constructively actually creates more problems and can lead to them derailing a negotiation process.[12]

A primary reason many people seek to keep emotions out of negotiation is because they are often brought into the process negatively and associated with disruption and anxiety. Many of us have experienced someone in a negotiation getting very angry or extremely despondent, and it is unnerving. However, as we have established, emotions are going to be involved, and certainly not all emotions are negative (think enthusiasm, passion, confidence, gratitude). So, ask yourself these questions:

1. What is my perspective on emotions in negotiation? Why?
2. If I think people should keep emotions out of negotiation, why do I hold that view?

3. Can I remember a time when I suppressed my emotions in my negotiations? Did it have the desired effect? If not, why not? And could I have expressed them differently, in a manner that could have kept the process moving forward?

4. When emotions arise, how can I view them differently? How might I view emotions not as negative, but as constructive drivers in negotiation?

Reach an Agreement at All Costs

There is a common misperception that the purpose of negotiation is to reach an agreement. While intuitively that might seem to make sense, upon further analysis it is misguided and something we need to unlearn. In most of our negotiations, it is not that difficult to reach an agreement. Think about it: We can always say yes to anything that will lead us there. What's difficult is to reach a really good agreement that *meets our objectives as best as possible*—which is the true aim of negotiation. If you think you might need to unlearn the purpose of negotiation, ask yourself these questions:

1. Why do I think the purpose of negotiation is to reach an agreement? Where did I learn that?

2. Can I think of a time where I reached an agreement only to realize that it did not really meet my objectives or goals?

3. Think of an instance when you did not reach an agreement (i.e., you walked away), and it was the right decision—why was that, and what can you learn from that experience?

A Win/Lose Mindset

Us versus them. This is when negotiations are a zero-sum game—someone has to win and someone has to lose. It's a fairly common mindset, but this is the worst way to approach a negotiation, particularly when we will be negotiating with that person or organization again in the future. Remember that negotiation is inherently an interdependent process, where both sides need the other to say yes to reach an agreement.

In my teaching and trainings, I frequently ask the participants the following question: What percentage of your negotiations are with the same people or organizations, time and again? Typically, the answer is between 85 and 90%. If that is the case, why would we see the other negotiator as our adversary? This mindset is self-defeating, for obvious reasons. For one thing, whichever party sees themselves as having "lost" will likely spend a great deal of time and energy trying to determine how to prevent that from happening in the next negotiation, or how to "get back at" the other party. This leads to many problems, including bringing animosity to the table, creating distrust, and an unwillingness to share information that might help you reach an agreement. Particularly in negotiations where you need to work with people over the long term, this is something negotiators must unlearn. Ask yourself:

1. Why do I hold the perception that the other negotiator is my adversary?
2. Does seeing the other negotiator as my adversary serve my interests? If so, how? If not, why not?
3. If I see negotiations as interdependent, can I imagine a different and more productive process? What might that process look like?

Both Parties Should Leave the Table a Little Unhappy

The mindset that the best negotiation is one where neither party is entirely satisfied in the end is something many of us must unlearn. A few years ago, I was at an academic conference where I met a friend of a friend who inquired as to what I did for a living. I explained that I engage in a lot of different kinds of negotiations, and I teach and train people in that realm. She seemed very interested and explained to me that she also negotiates a lot for her work. Then she proudly proclaimed, "To me, the best negotiation is when everyone leaves the negotiation table a little bit unhappy." I looked at her and asked, "Why do you hold that view?" She thought about it for a second or two and then stated, "Years ago one of my bosses told me that, and he was pretty successful, and so I adopted it as my mantra." I smiled and asked, "How do you think that mindset has worked for you over the years?" Surprised by the question, she blushingly replied, "OK . . . I guess. By the nature of your question, I'm sensing it may limit me in ways I hadn't considered." She seemed to get the idea without me saying anything more.

When everyone leaves the table a little unhappy, nobody ever meets their objectives optimally, so the process, at least subconsciously, can only end up being disappointing. This notion also sets the bar low—instead of striving for the best possible deal that might meet everyone's needs, we look for the least bad option and usually find it. If this is a perspective you might hold, ask yourself:

1. Why am I fine with the idea that I should leave the table a little unhappy? Where did I learn that?

2. What if I were to change my mindset to one focused on creative problem solving, where I don't look for any predetermined outcome, let alone a less than ideal one?

3. Can I think of negotiated agreements, either my own or that I have heard of, that were very good for both sides? Why can't that be my goal in the future?

Nature, Not Nurture, Is What Produces Great Negotiators

For many years I have heard people talk about how they were born to be great negotiators. To say I am a little skeptical of this notion is, to put it mildly, an overstatement. Like with any skill, we have to learn to become effective negotiators. Might some people be predisposed to engage in negotiations more easily than others? Perhaps, but that's where it stops. Let me explain it this way. I teach an introductory class in negotiation each semester. The common refrain in the evaluations, and in my discussions with the students at the end of the class, is how much they have learned and how their eyes have been opened to the many different nuances involved in negotiation. In short, exposing them to new concepts, different approaches, and new ways of thinking completely changes their perspective on negotiation in general and themselves as negotiators more specifically. If you think you were born a great negotiator, ask yourself:

1. Exactly what do you think you do in your negotiations that you did not learn at some point to do?

2. How do you determine which skills and abilities might be a result of nature versus nurture?

3. As you look back at your career, what have your experiences as a negotiator taught you, and how did that help you improve?

Intuition, Not Preparation, Is the Key to Success in Negotiation

Years ago, I was in Europe meeting with a group of negotiation experts about a specific conflict we were working on. While conversing with a very well-known negotiator who had many decades of experience, I asked him about how he prepared for negotiations. He explained that when he had gotten started in the field not as much was known about the importance of preparation and, in his words, he was a bit arrogant. He thought he could just feel his way through the process, engaging in his negotiations "by the seat of his pants," as he put it. He then explained how, as he gained more experience, he realized how wrongheaded that thinking was. "Intuition is very important," he said, "but it is a necessary—not sufficient—condition for success. It has to be coupled with effective and thoughtful preparation, or it's a sure recipe for failure." He admitted he had learned that the hard way. If you rely largely on intuition in your negotiations, ask yourself:

1. Why do I not feel the need to prepare? How did I learn that intuition was sufficient for success in negotiation?

2. Has my intuition ever let me down and caused me not to see things in a negotiation that I might have noticed had I been better prepared?

3. When I look back at my negotiations, in what ways could I have done better? How could preparation have helped me?

First Offers—Always and Never

A rule that I have in life is when people say "I always" or "I never," I immediately become wary. This is how I feel when people say they always or never make a first offer, and it's a behavior we need to unlearn. When I hear negotiators say this, the first question that comes to mind for me is "Are there never times when you do something different, depending on the situation or the context?" If you hold the view that as a negotiator you should always (or never) make a first offer, here are a few questions for you to contemplate:

1. Why do you always (or never) make a first offer? What is the thinking behind that?
2. Can you think of a time when your approach to first offers did not work out? If you had made a first offer (or waited), would that have changed the negotiation dynamic?
3. Under what conditions might you change your approach, and why?

As this relatively short list of ideas about negotiation that commonly need to be unlearned suggests, you likely have much to unlearn. Most of us have picked up various ideas and myths about negotiation that we've simply accepted as true without asking ourselves about them more deeply. These concepts may be getting in the way of our success and should be jettisoned for something better. I encourage you to think carefully about the core principles that guide your approach to negotiation and examine them in more detail, as we've done here. Are they serving you well as a negotiator, or maybe holding you back in ways you had not considered?

One succinct way to summarize this step is Stop, Start, Continue.[13] What will you *stop* doing that is getting in your way? What will you *start* doing next time that will replace what you are stopping? And what is working that you want to *continue* doing? Analyzing and addressing your weaknesses in this way will help you in your next step of getting back to the table smarter and stronger.

8

Step 5
Return to the Table
Smarter and Stronger

First of all, you never want to waste a failure. Adversity can break some people. Adversity can make some people great. It just depends on how you deal with it.

—NICK SABAN[1]

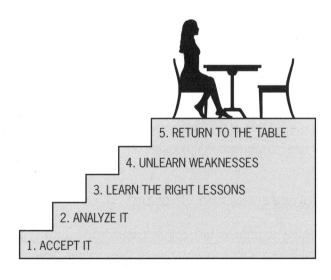

The previous steps have been about reflecting on negotiations that did not go as planned, coping with the frustration of a less-than-optimal outcome, truly learning from that specific experience, and examining our weaknesses and the stories we tell ourselves about who we are as negotiators. Or, in Saban's words, it has all been about never wasting a failure. This is not just an exercise; it's a way of setting ourselves up for success, as renewed and more insightful negotiators. What that means is that we return to the negotiation table smarter, stronger, and with greater confidence. That's the final step in our process.

Confidence is an elusive concept in general, and an equally evasive one when it comes to the realm of negotiation. In negotiations, we possess confidence when we feel that we have a good command of the situation and what is being discussed. When the negotiation drifts into an area where we lack knowledge, are uncomfortable with the subject matter (or the other negotiator), or are otherwise mired in uncertainty, we begin to feel less confident, and self-doubt creeps in. So, in addition to what we've already covered, what can we do to ensure we come back to the table with the confidence we need, and maintain it through as much of the negotiation process as possible? In this chapter, we'll look at the core elements that will help us return to the table confidently: self-awareness in managing the emotional aspects involved, increased knowledge of negotiation in general and the specific process we are about to reengage in, a new way to think about uncertainty, and the mindset and skills to adapt to new information that comes our way.

Self-Awareness and Emotions

The ability to possess and maintain confidence at the negotiation table begins with self-awareness. The previous steps in this framework have helped us to develop our self-awareness when things have not gone as planned and are certainly all applicable at this stage—but there's more to the story.

Self-awareness is also about maintaining a sense of self-control as the process unfolds. Emotions are an important aspect of this, and one that we have not yet discussed in great depth. Emotions play an important role in our negotiations, and the challenge is that when our emotions begin to overwhelm us, we have a problem. This is an all-too-familiar issue for most negotiators. As a participant in one of my trainings once stated to me, "If we could find a way to do away with emotions when we negotiate, it would be a lot easier!" Unfortunately, we cannot do that (and indeed, as discussed in the previous chapter, this is one of the concepts that I think negotiators should unlearn), so instead we have to learn to manage them. That does not mean suppressing them, but rather finding a way to bring them into the process constructively, so they are part of the process in a manner that can be addressed.

The best way to approach this challenge is by improving our emotional intelligence. A lot of wonderful work on this concept has been done by Daniel Goleman,[2] and investing some time in it is definitely worthwhile. In the meantime, I recommend a simple yet helpful technique, first elucidated by Ronald Heifetz and later by my colleague William Ury, called *going to the balcony*. Heifetz defines going to the balcony as "the mental activity of stepping back in the midst of action and asking—What's really going on here?"[3] Stepping back in this way not only helps us understand what is happening, but also has the dual purpose of temporarily removing us from the heat of the moment, thereby preventing our emotions from overwhelming us and enabling us to manage them effectively.

There are many types of balcony trips that I utilize, from quick ones that I take while still at the table—taking deep breaths or mentally imagining that I'm in a place of calm—to slightly longer ones where I step away for a break to get a coffee or go for a short walk. All of these can be very helpful in allowing us to keep our composure, while also experiencing (and not denying) the emotions we are feeling. A balcony trip can be longer, too: perhaps taking a day or two to think about an offer or proposal that is on the table that has a strong emotional component to it. The key is to step away, engage in some thought and introspection, ask ourselves why we are feeling a certain way, and then come back to the table more prepared and better able to manage our emotions effectively. As William Ury likes to say, "You have your emotions with some control, they don't have you."

I have been teaching people about going to the balcony for many years, and they constantly remark how valuable a technique it is to know about because the emotional dimension is so hard to handle effectively. As negotiators, making this a regular part of our repertoire will stand us in good stead. In short, when we feel our emotions beginning to take us over in an unhelpful manner, we should pause and step away, to avoid saying something that we might regret and that will make the challenge that much harder.

Increasing Our Knowledge of Negotiation

To be confident in negotiation we need to know a considerable amount about negotiation in general, including the various dynamics, process choices, and other hidden dimensions that might be impacting things. Many people who lack this knowledge understandably do not know to look for these elements. For example, certain aspects of a person's identity, such as race, gender, culture, or generation, may have a subtle (or not so subtle) effect on a negotiation process. An insightful negotiator will know to recognize when these factors might be driving behavior beneath the table. There are many wonderful books on negotiation and unconscious bias that can help us gain more knowledge, and it is essential to invest time and energy here. Of course, this knowledge has to be coupled with continued practice and the gaining of experience. There is no substitute for the yin-yang of theory and practice—it is the most powerful way to genuinely learn and grow.

Also vital to confidence is knowledge about the specific negotiation process in front of us, whether it's a new endeavor or one that we want to revive. In addition to general knowledge about negotiation, this has to do with preparation, as discussed previously, and comparing the negotiation with ones we've experienced in the past and looking for similar (or dissimilar) features. Once we have conducted that analysis, we need to get ourselves ready for the unknown aspects of the process—we know those exist, but we don't know what they are yet.

Uncertainty and the Necessity of Adapting

A common challenge for negotiators is having difficulty adapting to new and changing situations. Many of us are just not comfortable with this, or don't feel that we do it well. Unfortunately, there is no way around this challenge, so we have to push through it. To help with this, let me share a new way to think about uncertainty and provide some practical tips that you can apply to really work on your ability to adapt and develop a flexible mindset.

Start by seeing the world, and the negotiation situations you find yourself in, as inherently ever-changing. There's an old saying that "man plans and God laughs." Clearly, what that's getting at that is humans have a desire to plan and manage their way through life, but life (and negotiation!) throws many unexpected challenges at us. If we expect the unexpected, we train our minds to be open to that possibility.

Let's return to the notion of uncertainty that I touched on earlier, when discussing dealing with the grief associated with failure. For many, uncertainty has a negative connotation and is an uncomfortable space to exist in—but there is another way to think about it that can change our frame of mind. I think this perspective is exceedingly helpful for maintaining confidence during uncertain times in negotiations. Maggie Jackson, author of *Uncertainty: The Wisdom and Wonder of Being Unsure*, spoke with me about this possibility. To begin, it is important to point out that there are many definitions of uncertainty. In this case we are referring to psychological uncertainty, or the recognition of what we do not know. In her book, Jackson expresses the idea that "The best thinking begins and ends with the wisdom of being unsure."[4] In fact, she makes the case that uncertainty can fuel greatness because it plays an essential role in higher-order thinking, propelling us to new heights of creativity. She adds that when we are triggered by not knowing, it forces us out of our predictable cogitating patterns and jolts us into thinking outside the box and reaching for new possibilities.

This may all sound well and good, but you might want further proof. For that, Jackson persuasively relies on neuroscientific research. She explains that this type of uncertainty is not rooted in fear, but rather in what is called a good stress response. What that means is that people's minds are more alert during times of uncertainty. As Jackson notes, "Instability leads to stress hormones, which then releases powerful neurotransmitters to boost receptivity to new data, primes various brain regions to share information, and fires up cognitive circuits that flexibly control our focus."[5] So, believe it or not, our minds are actually more open to finding solutions and ready to pivot to something new when we are in this heightened state. Jackson concludes with this powerful point: "Uncertainty is wisdom in motion."[6] The key for us at this stage of the process is to embrace this new notion of uncertainty, unlearning the negative associations this feeling may have for us.

Jackson links the ability to sit with uncertainty with curiosity, and the progression appears to be a natural one. When we are curious, we are predisposed toward questions more than statements; we ask what is possible, and we uncover new and valuable information that may hold the key to a solution. Curiosity helps with the part of our negotiations that, as previously mentioned, we need to figure out as the process unfolds. We are much more likely to uncover that with a curious mindset than anything else. Curiosity is all about focusing on questions that we can ask and figuring out how we can learn what we don't know. Having a genuine curiosity about the other party helps move us from *your story* and *my story* to *our story* and demonstrates respect and likability . . . two great ways to help us make progress toward our objectives. Respect and likability lead to the ability to have a more open conversation and to be more persuasive to the other, thereby facilitating problem solving.

Problem solving is a core skill for maintaining confidence and adaptability. When we are focused on problem solving, we look for opportunity, and we can get around roadblocks with this kind of thinking. This approach pushes us to experiment with different ideas and predisposes us toward being adaptable, coming up with different solutions until we find one that works well.

Being adaptable requires us to train our minds to be agile, shifting from one concept to another and taking in new information as it emerges. One way to do that is to learn the skills of improvisation. For some practical insights on how to do this, I interviewed my colleague Izzy Gesell, who teaches improvisation in many different contexts. (Incidentally, the connection between negotiation and improvisation is fascinating, and a number of academics have explored this at some length.[7]) I asked Izzy if he could suggest some ways to strengthen or acquire skills specifically related to being adaptable. He began by explaining that to be adaptable one has to be firmly rooted in the present, so we can listen for opportunities for where to take a conversation. As negotiators, too often we are focused on the future and miss openings in the present to influence or change the direction of the conversation. So, the goal becomes to listen carefully and attentively for clues to what is going on and what could happen next, and then to let go of the desire to control the process (and sometimes, the outcome).

To demonstrate all of this, Izzy engaged me in an exercise that helps people grasp the uncertain nature of many of life's interactions. (See Appendix B for more on this and other exercises from Izzy that you can try out to work on your adaptability.) The exercise was called "One Word," and the essence was to create a story with one or more other people, each contributing one word at a time.[8] As we engaged in this exercise, I could see I how I was being forced to let go, not make assumptions about where the story would go, and co-own the process with him. It certainly felt a little uncomfortable at first, and my natural reaction was to try to think ahead, but then I slowed myself down and pushed myself to stay in the moment. When I did that, I became much more comfortable in the uncertainty of what was to happen and was able to adapt as the process unfolded. I learned that sitting in the present and taking the process as it comes was the key for me in being able to adapt more freely. This, as Izzy later explained, is exactly the idea, and it's something you will likely experience if you are able to try this exercise yourself.

Izzy then recounted a story from one of his trainings about the impact this exercise had had on a particular participant. He'd asked the group to carry out the "One Word" exercise without any time limits or constraints, and afterward, during the debriefing, this woman shared that she'd had an epiphany. As she and her colleagues played the game, she noticed that she was trying to hurry through it, despite the instructions to the contrary. She realized that everything in her work life had a time limit to it, so she was transferring that mindset to the game. She explained to Izzy that she now realized why her direct reports were so nervous every time they met with her. In her words, "Every interaction felt as if we were under the gun." In turn, this realization made her notice certain biases of hers that she hadn't recognized, and her tendency to try to get things done quickly in every situation, no matter the context. She also realized that she had to unlearn the habit of bringing this frenetic pace and energy to all her interactions and to stop trying to control every aspect of processes that, in certain ways, were out of her hands.

This story exemplifies what we need to do to be adaptable. Strengthening our ability to sit with uncertainty and stay in the present, while remaining adaptable, is essential to effective negotiation. While not easy, it is part of the journey of perpetual learning.

Shifting Our Focus to the Previous Negotiation and Reconnecting with the Other Negotiator

The following process will help us get back to the table and try to revive talks after a setback or recoverable failed negotiation. In these cases, it is important to reorient ourselves with where the previous process left off and to consider what the other negotiator might need to reengage. Let's look at these two dimensions to make certain we are ready for this challenge.

In the previous steps, we focused on learning from our failures—from both Forest and Trees vantage points—and the notion of transferring the right lessons to our future negotiations. Both of those are critical at this juncture. The next dynamic to consider is how to get back to the table when things ended poorly.

As we seek to reengage with the other negotiator, it can be helpful to reach out to them—regardless of how things ended— and put the onus on ourselves to try to restart talks. A reasonable question you might ask here is, well, what if the other negotiator was the difficult party? Why should we reach out to them? Shouldn't they come to us? To address this viewpoint, consider the story of Nelson Mandela. Most people know that Mandela, an activist, a politician, and ultimately a peacemaker, engaged in a prolonged struggle to free his country, South Africa, from apartheid rule. Mandela sacrificed greatly to achieve this goal, spending 27 years of his life in a prison on Robben Island, just off the South African coast. Upon his release, he reached out to the then President of South Africa, F.W. de Klerk, to begin negotiations. When a journalist asked why he did not wait for de Klerk to reach out to him given his long confinement, he answered that someone had to knock on the door first. The reasoning? In his words, "Resentment is like drinking poison and then hoping it will kill your enemies."[9] Surely, if Mandela could spend 27 years in prison, manage his feelings of deep resentment, and keep his eyes on the prize of freeing his nation, we can muster the strength to reach out and try to revive talks . . . no matter how difficult that may be.

When we come back together with the other negotiator for the first time, the opening conversation will likely have the potential to be awkward, but it will also be extremely important. One of the critical actions we can take is to acknowledge that the negotiation did not end where either party wanted. The taking of shared responsibility, avoiding any tinge of blame, is an important part of getting back to the table. From there, we want to focus on the lessons we learned and what will be persuasive to the other negotiator this time around.

As we seek to reengage with our counterpart, we should not assume that we will both pick up exactly where we left off. We need to reflect on where the other negotiator might be mentally as they come into this renewed negotiation and be prepared for some unexpected (or lingering) perspectives they may hold. This will help us reason about where the other negotiator may be now compared to where they were before in terms of their goals and objectives. We must also consider whether certain dynamics—for example, market conditions or power differentials—have changed in one direction or the other.

Once we have done this examination, we should spend some time thinking about what might be persuasive to the other negotiator, and why. Were there things we learned in the last process about what did or did not motivate them that we can draw on? A number of years ago I learned about Aristotle's three means of persuasion—*logos*, *pathos*, and *ethos*—and I have found that they provide a very helpful frame for trying to reconnect with the other party. Logos is the use of logic to make our case. So, we can ask ourselves, did the other negotiator seem to be most responsive to a logical case based on data or other factual information? If they were not moved by data or logic, perhaps pathos will connect with them more innately. Pathos is all about the emotional dimensions of a negotiation—fears, concerns, and passions. Here, it's important to consider how the other negotiator feels about the situation and the emotional connection between us and them. Often, stories or examples fit into this realm and speak to people much more clearly than impersonal facts. The third element, ethos, is about establishing our credibility and trustworthiness. Was that somehow a problem in the previous negotiation? If so, we might need to candidly consider whether we are the best messenger to get them back to the table. It might suit our objectives to add another negotiator to our team that adds a layer of credibility that was lacking in the eyes of the other negotiator.

A few years back, I shared this persuasion strategy with the participants of a negotiation training I was conducting with an engineering firm. During the break, a project manager (PM) at the firm came up to me and explained that she had found the idea of the three aspects of persuasion very interesting. Then she began to describe a negotiation problem she had been having with her counterpart from the City. They'd run into an issue four weeks earlier related to a construction project and soil contamination. The PM from the engineering firm had explained how they could fix the problem in some detail, but the PM from the

City was not convinced. The negotiation had dragged on with no solution in sight—but after hearing about the three means of persuasion, she thought she now knew where the problem lay. She was using a logos approach—very data-oriented—coupled with a lot of engineering jargon. She realized that the City's PM, who was relatively new to the field, might not have grasped all the information that she was throwing at her. As she recounted, "The City's PM kept saying, I still don't understand how this will solve the problem or how I will explain the change to the City Council." That's when it hit her that what might be driving her counterpart was some form of pathos, perhaps based on fear. She realized she needed to address that first before getting into the logos dimension, and she told me she would let me know how it went.

A week later, I found an email from her in my inbox with the heading "SUCCESS" (yes, in all caps). The PM shared that she had met with her counterpart a few days after the training and really focused on the emotional side of the problem. She had asked, "What is it that's keeping you up at night?" As she then told me, "The floodgates opened, and the PM shared all her worries and fears about the project. She was terrified of messing this up and did not really have the knowledge to understand if what I was proposing made sense." She then recounted how she had empathized with the City's PM, assuaged her fears, and then and only then walked her through the solution she was proposing, while also expressing her willingness to meet with the City Council along with her to answer any of their questions. She had broken through. The City's PM was very grateful, and they began to get the project back on track.

Looking out for what was driving her counterpart's behavior was the key in this interaction. Once she understood that better, she was able to tailor her approach to the right element of the logos, pathos, ethos framework. Usually, one of these will rise to the top in terms of importance during our negotiations, although all three often play a role at some point in the process. Awareness and knowing what to look for are critical to our ability to be persuasive.

Coming back around to the idea of restarting a previous negotiation process, it is now time to try to think through whether there was any helpful progress made there that can be built upon. Can we identify any places where, in hindsight, there may have been more overlap between our underlying interests than we initially realized, and thus more possibilities for moving forward? And finally, what can be done about the sticking points or challenges that caused the breakdown in the previous negotiation? Can we think of any fresh ideas for getting past those issues now? This may require some internal work with colleagues to brainstorm and think differently so we can make it easier for the other party to say yes.

Once we have done all of these things, we will feel more prepared and confident, knowing that we have considered what is different about the circumstances before we reengage, that we have thought about the situation from the other party's perspective, and that we have some new ideas about how to get over the hurdles that initially led to the setback or caused the negotiation to fail.

9

Looking Back to Look Ahead

Want to know the difference between a master and a beginner? The master has failed more times than the beginner has even tried.

—MEL ROBBINS[1]

Throughout this book, I have sought to address the understudied but all-too-familiar challenge of negotiations not turning out the way we hoped and planned. We have all experienced this over the course of our careers, and many of us have struggled to determine what to do when things go wrong. How do we cope? Do we brush off our failure to protect our reputation? Do we become so devastated by a significant setback or outright failure that we think of negotiation in general as an anxiety-producing event? Or do we roll up our sleeves, grapple with what happened, and truly learn from what has transpired in order to become better negotiators? My hope is that the last approach is where you have landed after reading this book, and that you understand the value of putting in the needed work.

This entire process reminds me of the ancient Japanese art of Kintsugi. Kintsugi, which is often called the art of embracing imperfection, is a traditional practice that has been around for many centuries. The art form involves repairing broken pottery pieces. But to fix the cracks, the artists don't just use any materials; rather, they use a special mixture of lacquer and a precious metal—gold, silver, or platinum. The idea behind Kintsugi is not to hide the breakages by repairing them so the cracks cannot be seen, but to celebrate them. The goal is to make the repaired piece even more beautiful than it was before. As such, Kintsugi symbolizes the Japanese philosophy of seeing imperfections not as flaws, but as something unique and beautiful.

Kintsugi can serve as a powerful analogy for us as negotiators. Each setback or failure creates a temporary crack in our view of who we are as a negotiator, but the 5 steps that have been discussed in this book provide a way of filling in these cracks, and repairing them in a way that makes us stronger. Rather than attempting to hide those scars, we should wear them openly, owning, understanding, and learning from our past failures and setbacks and recognizing that they have made us better negotiators.

My goal in writing this book was to provide a very realistic view of the process of negotiation. It is my sincere hope that your career is filled with far more successes than failures, but when failures come about, you are now equipped to do a number of important things to handle them effectively. As you have learned, the process of getting back to the table begins with thinking through the different categories of failure and understanding the magnitude of the setback you have experienced.

Then, you can grapple with the obstacles that might get in the way of learning from it and make sure they don't influence your perspective in a manner that leads you astray. It is at that point that you will put the 5 steps into practice.

In the first step, you have to genuinely accept that you experienced a significant setback or failure. This may not be easy, given the emotional dimensions involved and what you think this outcome says about you as a negotiator—but you must come to grips with it, or you will be blocked from progressing.

The second step is conducting a thorough big-picture (Forest) and micro (Trees) analysis to help you really understand what went wrong. Too often, our analysis stays in a comfortable place, but if we are going to genuinely learn from our missteps, we have to face the cold, hard facts of the situation.

It's then time to consider which of the lessons you've learned, both in terms of your behaviors and your attitudes, that you may be able to transfer from one negotiation to another. This third step requires a careful comparison, to help you avoid the classic mistake of transferring the wrong lessons from one negotiation to the next.

The fourth step is recognizing that your own weaknesses likely contributed to your failure. When we trace our weaknesses back to the core of where they came from, we usually realize that our internal story or some information that we have internalized about negotiation led us astray. We have to actively unlearn that information or viewpoint, and replace it with newer, more productive ways of approaching negotiation.

This unlearning sets up the last step in the process: coming back to the table smarter and stronger. To do that, you need confidence; you need to learn to exist more comfortably in uncertainty and develop your ability to adapt to new information that comes your way. And as you think about reviving talks and trying to get back to the table, you have to carefully consider what happened in the previous negotiation, what progress you can take away to build upon, and how you can constructively engage with your counterpart to bring them back to the table. Persistence and resilience will be essential at this juncture.

In the Introduction, I wrote about resilience and its importance, particularly when it comes to failure. Everything you have learned in this book has had the aim of making you a more resilient negotiator. In case it was not obvious, a growth mindset is essential in order to engage with the 5 steps and really underpins the process. And getting back up when negotiation knocks you down is really what we have been discussing all along. So, consider this book your template for resiliency, and practice, practice, practice.

Let me leave you with one final thought: Becoming a great negotiator is a journey, not a destination. Along that journey, as with most adventures, you will inevitably encounter many trials and tribulations, unexpected occurrences, and moments of joy, inspiration, and disappointment. However, in the end, if you embrace the ride, it will be one of the most rewarding endeavors of your lifetime. There will be times when you are deeply frustrated and feel as if you don't want to continue. That is where you will need to dig deep and stay the course. If you do, ultimately you will never be sorry, regardless of the outcome.

Appendix A

Additional Biases

Building on the discussion in Chapter 2, the following are some additional biases that often get in the way of our learning as negotiators (listed in alphabetical order):

- *Anchor bias* occurs when someone holds onto one initial piece of information and uses that as their entire basis for making decisions, to the exclusion of other data and relevant materials. This is a classic problem in negotiation and a common reason for failure in and of itself. In particular, if one party focuses too much on a single element of a negotiation they are likely to miss other information and details that are more or equally relevant and could help them succeed.

- *Conservatism bias* refers to the tendency to insufficiently revise one's beliefs when presented with new evidence. For example, when we take actions in a negotiation that lead us to failure, this bias can prevent us from learning from the experience and altering our perspective going forward, even if we're confronted with evidence that shows that a different course of action would have been more fruitful.

- *Entrapment*, also known as the sacrifice trap, is defined as "a decision-making process whereby individuals escalate their commitment to a previously chosen, though failing, course of action in order to justify or 'make good' on prior investments."[1] We see this a lot when it comes to failures in negotiation: one party chooses a particular course of action and has a very hard time altering their approach. This is often because, consciously or not, they want to avoid the embarrassment of admitting it was not the right one, but awareness of the time and costs that have been invested can also add to the challenge of changing course.

- *Optimism bias* causes us to overestimate the likelihood of positive outcomes. There is absolutely nothing wrong with having an optimistic outlook on negotiation and believing that you can reach an agreement with enough time, creativity, and hard work. In fact, much of the time, that's the best mindset to have. But optimism bias can also take hold in a manner that is unproductive, causing a negotiator to fail to prepare adequately and to trust that their past successes will enable them to meet their goals in their upcoming negotiations. While applying lessons learned from past experiences is one of the recommendations made in this book, as I have stressed, this must be done with great care and thought. There are often similarities between negotiations, but you must treat each one as a unique event, potentially with important differences in dynamics such as the negotiators' personalities and negotiation styles, power asymmetries, numbers of parties involved, and more.

- *Overconfidence* is a bias that impacts our ability to accept failure. Negotiators who fall victim to this bias tend to have excessive confidence in their decision-making and analysis skills. Ironically, this can manifest not only when we have a lot of experience in an area but also when we have very little. This bias gets in the way when we are trying to understand what has gone wrong, because our analysis causes us to draw conclusions that other factors were at play and the failure could not possibly have been due to us.

Appendix B

Improvisation Games from Izzy Gesell

The following five games will help you develop your ability to adapt and be flexible—a core skillset related to effective negotiation.

5 Fast Things

Objective: To freely associate five things related to a random topic within a flexible time limit.

 # Players: Unlimited

Time needed: 15–30 seconds per round

Process: Player 1 must name five things associated with the topic that is chosen by the group, in under 15 seconds. As they say each thing, the other players count loudly and show their fingers, "1, 2, 3, 4, . . ." At 5, all players attempt to say "And that's five things!" in unison, and the round ends.

Player 2 then is given a different category, and the game resumes.

Example: Player 1 is identified. The topic chosen is "emotions." As soon as a topic is named, Player 1 starts naming emotions: "love," "fear," "pleasure," "anger," "longing." The group counts off each emotion named. At five, all players attempt to say "And that's five things!" in unison, and the round ends.

Hints: The less thought given to each "thing," the more fun this game is. There is *no right answer.*

One Word at a Time (Also Known as "One Word" or "One Word Story")

Objective: Co-create a story that has never been told before.

 # Players: 2–6

Time needed: 2–5 minutes

Process: Players alternate adding one word at a time to the story. First, they choose a title of a story that has never been told. Player 1 starts by saying a word. Player 2 adds a second word, with the understanding that the players are working toward making sentences. Any player can add punctuation words ("period," "question mark," "exclamation point") to indicate the end of a sentence. The punctuation mark *does not* constitute that player's turn as adding a word. The game continues until it reaches a natural conclusion or one player says "The End."

Alphabet Game

Objective: Players work through the alphabet from A–Z, creating a dialogue where each successive contribution starts with a word beginning with the next letter.

 # Players: 2–6

Time needed: 2–5 minutes

Process: The first player begins their turn with a word that starts with the first letter of the alphabet, the second player begins with a word that starts with the next letter, and so on. The conversation continues until all the letters have been used.

Directions: Pick a topic that friends might talk about. This can be chosen by the audience or by one of the players. Player 1 begins the conversation with a sentence or two about that topic, making sure the first word they say starts with "A." Player 2 then picks up the conversation, starting with a word that begins with the letter "B." The game continues until all the letters have been used.

Example: Topic is "dieting." Player 1: "**A**ll diets are doomed to failure, because I always gain weight." Player 2: "**B**uy into the idea of lifestyle change and you may be successful." Player 1: "**C**arbs will be my downfall no matter what."

Variations: Begin with a random letter of the alphabet and complete the sequence ending with the letter right before the starting letter; start with "Z" and go backward.

Hints: This is not necessarily a "timed" game, so speed in answering is not required.

YES . . . AND/YES . . . BUT

Objective: Players co-create a blueprint for an agreed-upon project, such as a vacation or party.

 # Players: 2–6

Time needed: 2–3 minutes per round

Process: Players have a conversation or co-create a story by listening to each other, paraphrasing what is said, then either adding "AND" or "BUT" before contributing their own segment of the story or conversation. The game is played in two rounds: round 1 uses "Yes, and . . ." and round 2 uses "Yes, but . . ."

Round 1: Player 1 begins by making a statement. Player 2 says the word "YES," paraphrases what Player 1 said, adds the word "AND," then says whatever they would like to say. This continues until all players have had a chance to add to the conversation.

Round 2: Similar to round 1, substituting "AND" with the word "BUT."

Example: *Round 1*: Player 1: "I think it's too warm in here." Player 2: "YES, you think it's hot in here AND I am freezing so I wish they'd turn the heat up." Player 1: "YES, you want them to turn the heat up AND I'm happy to get you a blanket so you'll be warmer."

Round 2: Player 1: "I think it's too warm in here." Player 2: "YES, you think it's hot in here BUT I'm freezing so I wish they'd turn up the heat." Player 1: "YES, you're freezing BUT if they turn up the heat, I'll be even more uncomfortable."

Variations: Choose a topic to talk about before starting; make it competitive by losing points for using "BUT" when trying to say "AND."

Gibberish Poet

Objective: Working as a team and cooperatively, one player (the Gibberish Poet), speaking in gibberish, spontaneously creates a poem, and the other player (the Translator) spontaneously makes up a translation for the poem. Both players use words and physical movements as needed.

Players: 2

Time needed: Untimed

Process: Assuming the position and role of a poet reciting a poem to an audience, the Poet begins speaking in gibberish, using whatever intonation, pacing, and other vocal attributes or accompanying physical movements they like. The Translator, when cued by the Poet's pause or other indication, translates the gibberish into normal speech, using as many physical and tonal cues as possible to align the translation with the "feel" from the Poet. A pause or other indication by the Translator is a cue for the Poet to continue the poem.

Variations: Gibberish Expert, Gibberish Teacher, Gibberish Therapist. Gibberish Expert can be done with the expert topic chosen by the group or by one of the players. This game lends itself to many options.

Hints: Take cues and ideas from each other's movement, words, and intonation. Comedian Sid Caesar was a master of gibberish.

NOTES

Preface

1 Josh Howarth, "Startup Failure Rate Statistics," *Exploding Topics* (blog), November 3, 2023, https://explodingtopics.com/blog/startup -failure-stats#.

Introduction

1 Robert F. Kennedy, Day of Affirmation address, University of Cape-town, Capetown, South Africa, June 6, 1966, https://www.jfklibrary. org/learn/about-jfk/the-kennedy-family/robert-f-kennedy/robert-f -kennedy-speeches/day-of-affirmation-address-university-of -capetown-capetown-south-africa-june-6-1966.

2 Carol Dweck is the creator of the concept of fixed and growth mind-sets. Her book on the subject is entitled *Mindset: The New Psychology of Success* (New York: Ballantine Books, 2007).

3 Carol Dweck, "What Having a 'Growth Mindset' Actually Means," *Harvard Business Review Online*, January 13, 2016, https://hbr.org /2016/01/what-having-a-growth-mindset-actually-means.

Chapter 1

1 Jace Evans, "Giannis Antetokounmpo Says Bucks' Season Wasn't a Failure After Heat Loss," *USA Today*, April 27, 2023, https://www .usatoday.com/story/sports/nba/bucks/2023/04/27/bucks-giannis -antetokounmpo-says-season-not-failure-heat-upset/11749881002/.

2 It is also common to see this approach when it comes to the negotia-tions associated with peace processes to end wars. The parties know the challenge is daunting, but each process adds something to the ulti-mate solution. See examples from South Africa and Northern Ireland.

3 Brent Bambury, "The iPhone's Secret History: How Steve Jobs Went from Rejecting to Embracing the Future," *CBC Radio* (blog), June 23,

2017, https://www.cbc.ca/radio/day6/episode-343-the-iphone-s
-secret-history-prince-s-legacy-sustainable-weed-farming-and-more
-1.4173019/the-iphone-s-secret-history-how-steve-jobs-went-from
-rejecting-to-embracing-the-future-1.4173022.

4 Ibid.

5 Brian MacPherson, "Jon Lester: 'I Want to Be Here until They Have to
Rip This Jersey off My Back,'" *The Providence Journal*, January 23, 2014,
https://www.providencejournal.com/story/sports/mlb/2014/01/23
/20140123-jon-lester-i-want-to-be-here-until-they-have-to-rip-this
-jersey-off-my-back-ece/35377184007/.

6 Ricky Doyle, "Jon Lester 'Probably' Would Have Accepted $120M
Offer from Red Sox in Spring," *NESN*, December 14, 2014, https://nesn
.com/2014/12/jon-lester-probably-would-have-accepted-120m-offer
-from-red-sox-in-spring/. There are numerous other examples of this
kind of challenge in professional sports. Examples include Pedro Mar-
tinez's negotiations with the Red Sox and Lamar Jackson's with the
National Football League's Baltimore Ravens. For an important study
on this subject, see University of Technology Sydney, "In a Negotiation,
How Tough Should Your First Offer Be?" *ScienceDaily*, September 29,
2021, https://www.sciencedaily.com/releases/2021/09/210929101857
.htm. When it comes to first offers in general, also see Yola Engler and
Lionel Page, "Driving a Hard Bargain Is a Balancing Act: How Social
Preferences Constrain the Negotiation Process," *Theory and Decision* 93
(July 2022): 7–36, https://doi.org/10.1007/s11238-021-09835-y.

7 When I conduct training with representatives of governments, companies, and nonprofit organizations they frequently explain that approx-
imately 85–90% of their negotiations are with the same people or
organizations over and over again. So, the relationship almost always
matters and must be part of a negotiator's calculations.

8 A BATNA is what you will do if you cannot reach an agreement in a
given negotiation. If that happens, and you are at an impasse, what is
your best course of action? It's important to know your BATNA in any
negotiation so you have a point of comparison against which to judge
an offer in front of you. For more information on this subject see Brad
Spangler, "Best Alternative to a Negotiated Agreement," *Beyond Intrac-
tability* (blog), June 2003 (reviewed and updated in July 2012 by Heidi
Burgess), https://www.beyondintractability.org/essay/batna.

9 Frank Mastropolo, "When the Beatles Signed Their First Contract with Brian Epstein," *Ultimate Classic Rock* (blog), January 24, 2017, https://ultimateclassicrock.com/beatles-contract-brian-epstein/.

10 Ibid.

11 Dominic Utton, "The Beatles Lost Millions Because of Manager Brian Epstein's Blunders," *Express*, August 23, 2017, https://www.express.co.uk/life-style/life/844721/the-beatles-lost-millions-manager-brian-epstein-blunders.

12 Sim B. Sitkin, "Learning Through Failure: The Strategy of Small Losses," *Research in Organizational Behavior* 14 (January 1, 1992): 231–66.

Chapter 2

1 Goodreads, accessed August 2, 2024, https://www.goodreads.com/quotes/7987120-the-past-is-a-place-of-reference-not-a-place

2 Scott R. Peppet and Michael L. Moffitt, "Learning How to Learn to Negotiate," in *The Negotiator's Fieldbook: The Desk Reference for the Experienced Negotiator*, eds. Andrea Kupfer Schneider and Christopher Honeyman (Washington, DC: American Bar Association, 2006), 613–24. Other works on learning from negotiations include a chapter by Bruce Patton in *Teaching Negotiation: Ideas and Innovations*, ed. Michael Wheeler (Cambridge, MA: PON Books, 2000), and a short chapter by Jeff Weiss on reviewing your negotiations for lessons in his book *HBR Guide to Negotiating* (Cambridge, MA: Harvard Business Review Press, 2016). Finally, Dinnar and Susskind, in their book Entrepreneurial Negotiation: *Understanding and Managing the Relationships that Determine Your Entrepreneurial Success* discuss eight mistakes entrepreneurs make in their negotiations and how they tried to learn from them.

3 Oxford Learner's Dictionaries, s.v. "rationalization (*n.*)," accessed July 25, 2024, https://www.oxfordlearnersdictionaries.com/us/definition/english/rationalization.

4 Elizabeth A. Krusemark, W. Keith Campbell, and Brett A. Clementz, "Attributions, Deception, and Event Related Potentials: An Investigation of the Self-Serving Bias," *Psychophysiology* 45, no. 4 (July 2008): 511–15, https://doi.org/10.1111/j.1469-8986.2008.00659.x.

5 Itamar Shatz, "The Backfire Effect: Why Facts Don't Always Change Minds," *Effectiviology* (blog), Goodreads, accessed August 2, 2024, https://effectiviology.com/backfire-effect-facts-dont-change-minds/.

6 Goodreads, accessed August 2, 2024, https://www.goodreads.com/quotes/602588-uncertainty-is-an-uncomfortable-position-but-certainty-is-an-absurd

7 The Decision Lab, "Why Do We Buy Insurance? Loss-Aversion, Explained," https://thedecisionlab.com/biases/loss-aversion. Born out of work on loss aversion originally published by Daniel Kahneman and Amos Tversky (see Daniel Kahneman and Amos Tversky, "Prospect Theory: An Analysis of Decision Making Under Risk," *Econometrica* 47, no. 2 (March 1979), 263–92, https://doi.org/10.21236/ada045771).

8 This is a bias in and of itself called *entrapment*, where you get trapped by your own behavior due to sunk costs and not setting any limits. This often pushes us down roads we rationally should not go down, but we are blind to that reality and continue past a point that is rational so we can justify our behavior.

9 Interviewee preferred to remain anonymous. Interview by the author, March 18, 2022.

10 This quote is attributed to Kathryn M. Bartol, a management scholar and professor at the Robert H. Smith School of Business at the University of Maryland.

Chapter 4

1 Goodreads, accessed August 2, 2024, https://www.goodreads.com/quotes/661479-there-is-no-grief-like-the-grief-that-does-not

2 For some examples of challenges to this theory, see Hilda Bastian, "There Are No 'Five Stages' of Grief," *The Atlantic*, October 12, 2022, https://www.theatlantic.com/science/archive/2022/10/five-stages-complicated-grief-wrong/671710/, and Beth Tyson, "Debunking the Kubler-Ross Five Stages of Grief," *PACEs Connection*, November 7, 2022, https://www.pacesconnection.com/blog/debunking-the-kubler-ross-five-stages-of-grief.

3 Thanks to my colleague William Ury for alerting me to this notion.

4 As an aside, when I think of my own grief or loss acceptance, I see myself going through denial and anxiety and then acceptance and problem solving. I don't typically go through the stage of anger; it's just not something I need. The reason I raise this point is because it is important for you to analyze yourself and determine which stages are most relevant to you. This will make the process far more accurate. You need not contort yourself into a stage if you don't feel it applies to you.

5 Kenneth J. Doka and Terry L. Martin, *Grieving Beyond Gender: Understanding the Ways Men and Women Mourn*, rev. ed. (Boca Raton, FL: Routledge/Taylor & Francis Group, 2010).

6 eCondolence, "Fifth Stage of Grief: Acceptance," *eCondolence: The Resource for Condolences and Mourning* (blog), n.d., https://www.econdolence.com/learning-center/grief-and-coping/the-stages-of-grief/fifth-stage-of-grief-acceptance.

Chapter 5

1 Goodreads, accessed August 2, 2024, https://www.goodreads.com/quotes/106813-the-only-real-mistake-is-the-one-from-which-we

2 Thanks to my colleague William Ury for sharing this story with me.

3 Kimberlyn Leary, "Critical Moments in Negotiation," *Negotiation Journal* 20, no. 2 (April 2004): 143–51, https://doi.org/10.1111/j.1571-9979.2004.00012.x.

4 Deborah Kolb and Judith Williams, *The Shadow Negotiation* (New York: Simon & Schuster, 2000).

5 Anonymous interview with a colleague who is an expert in sales negotiation, Interview by the author, April 21, 2024.

6 Deborah M. Kolb, "Making Connection as Critical Moves in Negotiation," *Negotiation Journal* 36, no. 2 (Spring 2020): 193–206, https://doi.org/10.1111/nejo.12315.

Chapter 6

1 The John Maxwell Company, "Borrowing Experience," October 6, 2011, https://www.johnmaxwell.com/blog/borrowing-experience/.

2 The connection between negotiation and transference was first laid out by Susan Fukushima in 1999. See Susan Fukushima, "What You Bring to the Table: Transference and Countertransference in the Negotiation Process," *Negotiation Journal* 15, no. 2 (April 1999): 169–80, https://doi.org/10.1111/j.1571-9979.1999.tb00189.x.

3 I am admittedly using the term transference in a slightly different way than a therapist would use it, but there is some important applicability here that goes beyond just transferring lessons, because much of this has to do with our past experiences and how those are clouding what we are doing in our present negotiations.

4 Mark Pines, "What Is Transference? What to Do When It Shows Up in Therapy," *Open Counseling* (blog), March 3, 2022, https://blog.opencounseling.com/what-is-transference/.

5 For more information, see Kilmann Diagnostics, "An Overview of the TKI Assessment Tool," accessed August 2, 2024, https://kilmanndiagnostics.com/overview-thomas-kilmann-conflict-mode-instrument-tki/.

Chapter 7

1 Goodreads, accessed August 2, 2024, https://www.goodreads.com /quotes/107163-if-you-always-do-what-you-have-always-done-you

2 The media is a primary source I would point to for learning about negotiation, but there are various somewhat outdated sources that can cause problems. As one example, see Matt Gavin, "Bad Negotiation: 9 Mistakes to Avoid at the Bargaining Table," *Harvard Business School Online Business Insights Blog*, November 20, 2018, https://online.hbs .edu/blog/post/negotiation-strategies-what-not-to-do.

3 *Assertive* is defined here as "the quality of being self-assured and confident without being aggressive to defend a right point of view." Source: Wikipedia contributors, "Assertiveness," *Wikipedia: The Free Encyclopedia*, accessed August 2, 2024, https://en.wikipedia.org/wiki/Assertiveness.

4 Jeff Shore, "These 10 Peter Drucker Quotes May Change Your World," *NBC Business News* (blog), September 16, 2014, https://www.nbcnews .com/id/wbna56060818.

5 Paul Taylor, "Learning to Learn," *Forbes*, May 19, 2017, https://www .forbes.com/sites/sap/2017/05/18/learning-to-learn/.

6 Iowa State University Social Self and Culture Lab, "Cultures of Honor," accessed August 2, 2024, https://social.psych.iastate.edu/about-my -research/research-on-culture-of-honor/.

7 For a very good overview of the downsides of compromise, see Scott Van Soye, "What Typically Happens When You Compromise During a Negotiation?" *ADR Times* (blog), March 7, 2023, https://www.adrtimes .com/what-typically-happens-when-you-compromise-during-a -negotiation/.

8 For more information on the role of compromise and negotiation please see the following articles: https://www.forbesindia.com/article /mentors-and-mavens/compromise-should-be-the-last-decision-not -the-first-joshua-n-weiss/84071/1 and https://www.linkedin.com/pulse /deeper-dive-compromise-negotiation-getting-more-nuanced-joshua -weiss-zkfce/?trackingId=qHPdGw1S6175NbPbm9jkfQ%3D%3D.

9 Modified and adapted from https://fearlessculture.design. The Cycle
of Unlearning was created by Gustavo Razzetti (Creative Commons
Attribution 4.0 International License, https://creativecommons.org
/licenses/by/4.0/). Original source: Gustavo Razzetti, "The Power of
Unlearning: How to Let Go of Beliefs to Embrace Success," March 16,
2023, https://www.fearlessculture.design/blog-posts/the-power-of
-unlearning-how-to-let-go-of-beliefs-to-embrace-success.

10 Roger Fisher, William Ury, and Bruce Patton, *Getting to Yes: Negotiating Agreement Without Giving In*, 3rd rev ed. (New York: Penguin
Books, 2011).

11 Some people ask about cultural considerations when it comes to
emotions in negotiation. Those are certainly important to keep in
mind. However, all people, regardless of culture, experience emotions
at the negotiation table. The question is actually more about if it is
appropriate to express them or not. That is a more nuanced question
and a bit different from what I am asking you to unlearn.

12 See for example Roger Fisher and Daniel Shapiro, *Beyond Reason:
Using Emotions as You Negotiate* (New York: Penguin Books, 2006).

13 I am grateful to Izzy Gesell for sharing this short mantra with me.

Chapter 8

1 On3, "Nick Saban Reveals His Message to Alabama Players after Loss
to Texas," September 14, 2023, https://www.on3.com/college/alabama
-crimson-tide/news/nick-saban-reveals-message-to-alabama-players
-after-loss-to-texas/.

2 See for example Daniel Goleman, *Emotional Intelligence: Why It Can
Matter More Than IQ* (New York: Bantam Dell, 1995).

3 Mariam Rowhani, "Important Leadership Tips: Move Away from the
Dance Floor to the Balcony," *New Level Work* (blog), April 6, 2021,
https://www.bettermanager.co/post/move-away-from-the-dance
-floor-to-the-balcony.

4 Maggie Jackson, *Uncertain: The Wisdom and Wonder of Being Unsure*
(Gilford, CT: Prometheus Books, 2023), 7.

5 Ibid, 55.

6 Ibid, 45.

7 See for example Frank J. Barrett, *Yes to the Mess: Surprising Leadership Lessons from Jazz* (Cambridge, MA: Harvard Business Review Press, 2012), and Michael Wheeler, *The Art of Negotiation: How to Improvise Agreement in a Chaotic World* (New York: Simon & Schuster, 2013).

8 If you are having a hard time finding someone to do this exercise with or prefer to practice with a little more anonymity, you can use the new AI tool Khanmigo, available at https://www.khanmigo.ai . You can interactively create a story with the AI tool, by adding a word and the AI doing the same one at a time. It's very good practice for thinking quickly on your feet and learning to adapt.

9 *Los Angeles Times*, "Nelson Mandela Transformed Himself and Then His Nation," December 6, 2013, https://www.latimes.com /opinion/topoftheticket/la-xpm-2013-dec-06-la-na-tt-nelson-mandela -20131206-story.html.

Chapter 9

1 Mel Robbins (@melrobbins), post, March 19, 2018, 11:53 pm, accessed 2 August 2024, https://x.com/melrobbins/status/975867765566459911.

Appendix A

1 Joel Brockner and Jeffrey Z. Rubin, *Entrapment in Escalating Conflicts* (New York: Springer-Verlag, 1985), 5.

ACKNOWLEDGMENTS

In any work such as this, there are many people to thank. The time it takes to write a book is significant, and it requires a strong support network. This network begins with my immediate family—my wife Adina and daughters Kayla, Aylee, and Talya. You inspire and challenge me to try to live up to the principles that I teach to others. To my dad, thank you for always pushing me to be a lifelong learner and to keep challenging myself. You helped me build in myself the resilience that is so necessary in negotiation. To my sister Ilana and my brother-in-law Greg, thank you for your curiosity, conversations, and support over the years. To my relatives on my wife's side of the family—my father-in-law Mark, stepmother-in-law Wendy, brother-in-law Adam, sister-in-law Susan, brother-in-law Barry, and all of my wonderful nieces and nephews and their spouses (Jared and Shaleah, Rachel and Jeremy, Rebecca and Nir, Sarah and Yair, and Hannah and Michaela)—thank you for the encouragement, feedback, curiosity, and valuable questions.

I am deeply indebted to my negotiation colleagues for the community they have let me be part of and for sharing their ideas and thoughts with me about the book and its nuances. The Program on Negotiation community continues to inspire me and help me grow as a negotiator. Very personally, I want to thank a number of individuals in the negotiation world. I have listed them in alphabetical order: Kwame Christian, Calvin Crustie, Elizabeth Doty, Sheila Heen, Keld Jensen, Barney Jordan, David Lax, Melissa Manwarring, Shane Ray Martin, Felix Miller, Joe Navarro, Mark Raffan, James Sebenius, Daniel Shapiro, Lawrence Susskind, Scott Tillema, and William Ury.

To my book reviewers, Brian Abrams, Brian Blancke, Simon Blattner, Bob Cohen, Tracy Mazuer, and James Wylde, I thank you deeply for your time, effort, and insights, which helped improve the book as it took shape.

Thanks to Sophia Sampson, who helped me with the core graphic related to the 5-step process. She was very patient with me and easy to work with. I appreciate her help very much.

Finally, to the team at Berrett-Koehler—in particular, Jeevan Sivasubramaniam, Rachel Head, Katelyn Keating, Catherine Lengronne, Christy Kirk, Sarah Nelson, Robert Fox, and Ashley Ingram—I thank you so very much for all your time and effort in helping to make this book be the best it could be. Your attention to detail, interest in the project, constructive pushing back, and insights related to the publishing world were invaluable. This is the type of experience I was hoping for when I signed on with you.

INDEX

A

accepting failure, 10, 44, 49–58
accommodating style, 85
active unlearning, 88–89, 91–92, 96
adaptability, 7, 111–116, 129
adversarial mindset, 79, 101
adversity, 107
agenda setting, 67
agreement
 bad, 23–25
 imminent possibility of, 17–19
 as purpose of negotiation, 2
 unlearning mindset about, 100
 unmet objectives amidst, 19–21
always/never mindset, 105
analysis
 in 5-step process, 44
 of big/small picture, 11, 45, 59
 of the dark/difficult areas,
  59–60
 learning via, 40
 of ourselves, 34
 as a skill set, 8
 and unlearning, 88–91, 92
 What Went Wrong Worksheet,
  72–73
anchor bias, 125
anger, blame and, 34–36, 52, 54
Antenakupo, Giannis, 14

anxiety, 5, 50, 51, 54, 99
assertiveness, 8, 91
attitudes. *See* mindsets
avoiding style, 85
awareness, 92, 96, 108–110, 120

B

backfire effect, 37–38
Bad Agreement failures, 23–25
Bartol, Kathryn M., 41, 76
BATNA (Best Alternative to a
 Negotiated Agreement), 24,
 32, 53
behavior
 awareness of problematic, 92
 changing, 76, 86, 90
 to stop, start, and continue,
  106
 unlearning, 92–94
Bennett, Roy T., 33
biases, 34, 36–39, 40, 111, 115,
 125–127
big-picture analysis, 61–62, 71
blame
 avoiding, 117
 denial/rationalization and, 4
 as obstacle to learning, 34–36
breakdown of negotiations, 31–32
breaks, taking, 69–70

C

catastrophic failures, 32
certainty, 38, 52
challenges, facing
    emotional, 26
    and framing/reframing
      moves, 68
    vs. hidden dynamics, 27–28
    importance of, 42
    magnitudes of failure, 29–32
    obstacles to, 34–42
    practicing skills for, 8
    via "taking a crack at it,"
      16, 31
change of action, 5
collaborating style, 85
competing style, 85
compromise, 94, 98–99
compromising style, 85
confidence
    via 5-step process, 46
    coming back to the table
      with, 108
    importance of, 9
    via knowledge, 12
    lack of, 5
    overconfidence, 5, 127
    for problem solving, 113
    for resilient negotiation, 6
    to think on your feet, 8
    uncertainty and, 112
conflict solution, 2
conservatism bias, 125
control, relinquishing, 114
coping with failure
    as first post-failure step, x–xi,
      5, 10
    giving time for, 57–58
    importance of, 51
    obstacles to, 34–42
    recognizing and coping, 13
creative thinking, 32, 95, 112
credibility, establishing, 118
critical moments, 62, 63, 65, 67, 71
criticism, receiving, 36
cultural context
    in comparing negotiations, 86
    effects on negotiation, 111
    grief and, 53
    and unlearning, 92–93
curiosity, 113
customer relationships, 21–23, 79

D

daring, 1
deadlines/time pressures, 86, 94
deadlocks, 31
deals
    achievable, 17–19
    last-minute changes to, 27
    as purpose of negotiation,
      2–3
    unlearning mindset about, 100
Decision Lab, 40
defensiveness, 37–38
denial, 4, 14, 51
detail-oriented analysis, 61, 71
devaluation, reactive, 39
difficult conversations, 2, 8–9
disrespect, 27, 63–64
diverting moves, 69
Doka, Kenneth, 53
Drucker, Peter, 91
Dweck, Carol, 6
dynamics, hidden, 27–29, 111

E

ego, backfire effect and, 38

Emotionally Unintelligent failures, 26–27
emotions
    after failures, 11
    blame, 34–36
    disrespect for, 63–64
    emotional intelligence, 9, 109
    emotion-based failures, 26–27
    of grief, 49–56, 112
    and intentional pauses, 109–110
    negative, 99
    and negative transference, 83
    as part of life/negotiation, 99–100, 119
    and self-awareness, 108–110
    suppressed, 99
engineer mindset, 60–61
entrapment, 126
Epstein, Brian, 24–25
escalation, 70
ethos, 118
experience
    evaluating, 75
    and self-image, 87–88
    and self-reflection, 39–40
    and transference, 78
    and trust of intuition, 104

F

failures
    5-step process for learning from, 10–12, 43–47, 123–124
    causes of, 15
    coping. *See* coping with failure
    and daring greatly, 1
    defined, 13
    dwelling on, 4
    examining your, 10
    facing, 5, 13
    fear of, 14, 40
    learning from. *See* learning; lessons, learning
    likelihood of, 16
    magnitudes of, 9, 29–32, 62
    as an opportunity, 43
    as part of life/negotiation, ix–x, 5, 15
    reasons for, 88
    responses to, 4–5, 121–122
    vs. stepping stones to success, 14, 31
    types of, 9, 15–29, 62, 71
Fearless Design, 96
first offers, 105
fixed mindset, 6, 7, 8
flexibility, 129
Ford, Henry, 59
framework, lack of, 41–42
framing moves, 67

G

generational differences, 86
Gerjuoy, Herbert, 92
Gessell, Izzy, 114, 129–133
Getting to Yes, 98
goals, met/unmet, 13, 18, 19, 100
Goleman, Daniel, 109
Golidlocks and failure responses, 4–5
greediness narratives, 91
grief, 49, 112
Grieving Beyond Gender, 53
growth mindset, 6–8

H

habit formation, 96, 97

hard work, 7
Harrison, Stephanie, 83
Heifetz, Ronald, 109
heuristics, 36–39
honesty with ourselves
    blame vs., 34
    discomfort of, 91
    and facing failure, 14
    vs. self-serving bias, 37
honor culture, 93
hormones, stress, 113

I

identity
    effects on negotiation, 111
    failures involving our, 3
    protecting your, 34
impatience, 63–65
imperfection, embracing, 122
improvisation, 114, 129–133
influence, 9, 114
information, incomplete
    and the backfire effect, 38
    and invisible dynamics, 27–29
    as negotiation variable, 2
    and quick thinking, 7–8
intelligent failures, 30–31
intent and impact problem, 66, 70
interrupting moves, 69–70, 110
intuition, 104–105
Ive, Jonathan, 16

J

Jackson, Maggie, 112
Jobs, Steve, 16–17

K

Kennedy, Robert F., 1
Kintsugi, 122
Kirkpatrick, Jane, 87

knowledge/information
    of/about ourselves, 34
    and the backfire effect, 38
    confidence via, 12
    for effective negotiation, 9
    as engineer's comfort zone,
      60–61
    vs. hidden dynamics, 27–29
    increasing our, 110–111
    lack of, 25
    for resilient negotiation, 6
    unlearning/relearning, 87–106
Kolb, Deborah, 67
Kübler-Ross, Elisabeth, 50
Kübler-Ross model, 50–51, 53–54

L

last-minute changes, 27
learning
    5-step process for, 43–47
    continual, 5, 9
    from experience, 39, 47
    from failures, ix, 4, 6, 45, 88
    growth mindset, 6–8
    via intelligent failures, 30–31
    vs. self-serving bias, 37
    and unlearning, 11–12, 44,
      45–46, 88–106
lessons, learning
    5-step process for, 43–47
    analysis for, 59–73
    obstacles to, 34
    and owning failures, 14
    and resilient negotiation, 5
    right vs. wrong, 11, 44, 45, 75–86
    systematic approach to, 41,
      44, 47
    via "taking a crack at it," 16
    in a timely way, 43, 61
    value of, x, xi

Lester, Jon, 18–19
leverage, failure to use, 25
listening, 114
logos, 118
Longfellow, Henry Wadsworth, 49
long-term relationships, 21, 23, 79–80, 84
loss
    accepting, 44, 49
    aversion to, 40–41

M

macro critical moments, 63, 65, 71
magnitudes of failure, 9, 29–32, 62
Mandela, Nelson, 116–117
manipulation, 79
Martin, George, 24, 25
Martin, Terry, 53
Maxwell, John C., 75
Merchant, Brian, 16
micro critical moments, 63, 67, 71
mindsets
    adversarial, 79
    applying correct, 76
    changing via unlearning, 90, 97–98
    of compromise, 94
    of curiosity, 113
    and emotion following failures, 11
    of engineers, 60–61
    flexible, 111
    growth and fixed, 6–8
    heuristics and, 39
    loss aversion as, 40
    transference of, 80, 86
minimizing failures, 14
mistakes
    avoidable, 3
    avoiding repeated, 45

celebrating, 122
learning from, 88
repeated, 5, 76
Moffitt, Michael, 34
moves/turns in negotiation, 62, 63, 67–70
multiple-issue negotiations, 84

N

naming moves, 70
nature/nurture question, 103–104
negative transference, 81, 83
negotiation
    5 steps to improved, 43–47
    assertiveness in, 91
    compromise and, 94–95
    and continual learning, 5
    core skills for, 8–9
    dynamics in, 2, 11, 15, 27–29, 77, 84–86
    failure as part of, x, 15
    getting back to table for, 12
    handling modes/styles in, 85
    improving your, 2, 8, 88
    improvisation and, 114
    mindsets to unlearn for, 97–106
    moves/turns in, 62, 63, 67–70
    number of parties in, 84
    purpose of, 2–3, 100
    renewing, 116–120
    responses to failed, 4–5
    team alignment, 77
    uniqueness of each, 41–42, 76
negotiation partner
    comparing/contrasting, 85
    focus on, 46
    reception of moves/turns, 68
    reengaging with, 116
    underlying values of, 98–99

never/always mindset, 105
normalizing failures, x

O

objectives, met/unmet, 13, 18, 19,
    100, 102
obstacles
    to learning from failures,
        34–42
    overcoming, 7
    unhelpful mindsets, 97–106
*The One Device: The Secret History
    of the iPhone*, 16
One Word exercise, 114–115, 130
opening moves, 63
optimism bias, 126
overconfidence, 127
overthinking, 5
owning your failures, 14, 45

P

partnership, building, 2
pathos, 118
Penny-Wise and Pound-Foolish
    failures, 21–23
Peppet, Scott, 34
persuasion, 9, 114, 117–120
positivity, 14
power asymmetries, 32
preparation
    intuition vs., 104–105
    lack of, 24, 25
    as a skill set, 8
problem solving
    compromise vs., 95, 98
    as a core skill, 8, 113
    via open conversation, 113
    in stages of grief, 52–53, 54
    transference's effect on, 81

procrastination, 43
pushback, 37–38

Q

quick thinking, 7

R

rationalizing behavior, 4, 34, 36,
    37, 57
reactive devaluation, 39
reengagement, 116
reframing moves, 68
relationships
    building of, 2
    and curiosity, 113
    damage done to, 21–23, 32
    hidden dynamics in, 28–29
    long-term, 21, 23, 79–80,
        84, 101
    negotiating in new, 82
relearning, 96, 97
renewing negotiations, 116–120
reputation, 4, 36, 50, 52, 93
resentment, 117
resilience
    and improved negotiation, 2
    and learning from failure, xi,
        5, 9
respect, 3, 27, 113
Robbins, Mel, 121

S

Saban, Nick, 107
sacrifice trap, 126
sadness, 52, 55
sales negotiation, 69–70, 79, 81
second-guessing, xi
security, false sense of, 76
self-awareness, 108–110

self-image, 87–88
self-reflection, 34, 39–40,
    88–91
self-serving bias, 37, 38
setbacks, 13, 31, 88, 122
severity of failures, 9, 29–32
The Shadow Negotiation, 67
shock, 51
short-term gain, 21, 23, 79–80
single-issue negotiations, 84
Sitkin, Sim, 30
skill sets
    5-step negotiation process,
        43–47
    and adaptability, 114
    applying correct, 76
    core negotiation skills, 8–9
    improvisation, 114
    practice of new, 96, 97
    quick thinking, 7–8
    for resilient negotiation, 6
Slipping Through Our Fingers
    failures, 17–19
stalemates, 31
startup success rate, xi
stepping back, 109
sticking points, identifying, 46
stress response, 112–113
subconscious bias, 36
success
    and acceptance of loss, 58
    achievable, 17–19
    failures and, ix–x
    and growth mindset, 6
    via preparation, 104
    pressure for, x
    pursuit of, xi, 57
    setting yourself up for, 108
surviving failure, x

T

table, getting back to
    5 steps for, 10–12, 43–47,
        123–124
    and adaptability/uncertainty,
        111–116
    clear path to, 31
    confidently, 108
    with increased knowledge,
        110–111
    meaning of, 12
    persuasiveness and,
        116–120
    self-awareness of emotion in,
        108–110
tact, 70
tactics, correcting, 76
Take a Crack at It failures,
    16–17
team alignment, 77
temporary setbacks, 31
thinking
    creative, 32, 53, 95, 112
    flexible, 111, 129
    mindsets to unlearn, 86,
        97–106
    overthinking, 5
    quickly/on your feet, 7
    and the stress response,
        112–113
    subconscious, 83, 90, 91
Thomas-Kilmann model, 85
time pressures/deadlines, 86, 94
tipping points, 63
transference, 77–83
trust
    amidst uncertainty, 114–115
    and distrust, 27, 29
truth, confronting, 51

turning points, 63
turns/moves in negotiation, 62, 63,
    67–70

U

uncertainty
    accepting, 46
    and adaptability, 111–116
    anxiety about, 51–52
    discomfort of, 38
    managing, 12
    wisdom of, 112–113
*Uncertainty: The Wisdom and
    Wonder of Being Unsure,* 112
understanding failure, 5
Under the Table failures, 27–29

unexpected situations, 112
unlearning, 5, 11–12, 44, 45–46,
    88–106
Ury, William, 109, 110

V

Voltaire, 38

W

walkaway alternatives, 24
weaknesses, improving, 87–91, 106
What Were You Thinking failures,
    19–21
Wheeler, Michael, 63
Williams, Judith, 67
win/lose approach, 79, 80–81, 101

ABOUT THE AUTHOR

D r. Joshua N. Weiss is cofounder, with William Ury, of the Global Negotiation Initiative at Harvard University and a senior fellow at the Harvard Negotiation Project. He is also the director and creator of the Master of Science in Leadership and Negotiation degree program at Bay Path University. He received his PhD from the Institute for Conflict Analysis and Resolution at George Mason University in 2002.

In his current capacity he conducts research, consults with many different types of organizations, delivers negotiation and mediation trainings and courses, and engages in negotiation and mediation at the organizational, corporate, government, and international levels. He has conducted trainings and consulted with organizations, companies, and governmental entities including the Canadian government, CDM Smith, Christie's auction house, Deloitte, General Motors, Genzyme, Harvard University, Houghton Mifflin Harcourt Publishing, the Massachusetts Institute of Technology, Mass Mutual, Microsoft, the United Auto Workers, the United Nations (Mediation Unit, UNAOC, UNITAR, and UNDP), the United States government (State Department, Federal Emergency Management Agency, National Park Service, and Transportation Security Administration), Yale University, and various state governments.

Joshua has published a number of influential books over the course of his career. The first were the *Negotiator in You* series of audio books published by BBC Broadcasting, which included four different books on negotiating at work, at home, and in the world around you, with a special edition for salespeople. These were followed by *The Book of Real-World Negotiations: Successful Strategies from Business, Government, and Daily Life*, published by Wiley Press in 2020. Rather than discussing hypothetical scenarios, that work highlights real-world negotiation examples, revealing what is possible through preparation, persistence, creativity, and taking a strategic approach to negotiation. In addition, he delivered a TED Talk in 2018 entitled "The Wired Negotiator" about the role of technology in negotiation and how to use it most effectively.

Berrett–Koehler
Publishers

Berrett-Koehler is an independent publisher dedicated to an ambitious mission: *Connecting people and ideas to create a world that works for all.*

Our publications span many formats, including print, digital, audio, and video. We also offer online resources, training, and gatherings. And we will continue expanding our products and services to advance our mission.

We believe that the solutions to the world's problems will come from all of us, working at all levels: in our society, in our organizations, and in our own lives. Our publications and resources offer pathways to creating a more just, equitable, and sustainable society. They help people make their organizations more humane, democratic, diverse, and effective (and we don't think there's any contradiction there). And they guide people in creating positive change in their own lives and aligning their personal practices with their aspirations for a better world.

And we strive to practice what we preach through what we call "The BK Way." At the core of this approach is *stewardship,* a deep sense of responsibility to administer the company for the benefit of all of our stakeholder groups, including authors, customers, employees, investors, service providers, sales partners, and the communities and environment around us. Everything we do is built around stewardship and our other core values of *quality, partnership, inclusion,* and *sustainability.*

This is why Berrett-Koehler is the first book publishing company to be both a B Corporation (a rigorous certification) and a benefit corporation (a for-profit legal status), which together require us to adhere to the highest standards for corporate, social, and environmental performance. And it is why we have instituted many pioneering practices (which you can learn about at www.bkconnection.com), including the Berrett-Koehler Constitution, the Bill of Rights and Responsibilities for BK Authors, and our unique Author Days.

We are grateful to our readers, authors, and other friends who are supporting our mission. We ask you to share with us examples of how BK publications and resources are making a difference in your lives, organizations, and communities at www.bkconnection.com/impact.

Dear reader,

Thank you for picking up this book and welcome to the worldwide BK community! You're joining a special group of people who have come together to create positive change in their lives, organizations, and communities.

What's BK all about?

Our mission is to connect people and ideas to create a world that works for all.

Why? Our communities, organizations, and lives get bogged down by old paradigms of self-interest, exclusion, hierarchy, and privilege. But we believe that can change. That's why we seek the leading experts on these challenges—and share their actionable ideas with you.

A welcome gift

To help you get started, we'd like to offer you a **free copy** of one of our bestselling ebooks:

www.bkconnection.com/welcome

When you claim your **free ebook**, you'll also be subscribed to our blog.

Our freshest insights

Access the best new tools and ideas for leaders at all levels on our blog at ideas.bkconnection.com.

Sincerely,

Your friends at Berrett-Koehler